CW01192842

William Hazlitt is one of the great English essayists. He was born in 1778 in Maidstone, Kent. Soon after, the Hazlitt family went briefly to America before settling in Wem, Shropshire, where Hazlitt's father became a Unitarian preacher. As a young man Hazlitt followed his father into the ministry but lost his faith. After failing in his ambition to become a portrait painter, he took a job as journalist with one of the most important daily newspapers of the day, the *Morning Chronicle*. He had discovered his calling as one of the most courageous writers of his time, unafraid of attacking powerful figures including the poet laureate, politicians, even the king. In the course of a career that lasted less than three decades, he wrote some of the finest literary journalism, art criticism, sports commentary, and theatrical reviews of the Romantic period. Had it not been for him, the conversational essay we know today would not exist. Though he enjoyed considerable fame, he died in poverty and relative obscurity in Frith Street, London, in 1830.

Duncan Wu was a postdoctoral Fellow of the British Academy (1991–4), and Professor of English Literature at the Universities of Glasgow (1995–2000) and Oxford (2000–8). He is currently Professor of English at Georgetown University in Washington, DC. His biography, *William Hazlitt: The First Modern Man*, was published by Oxford University Press in 2008.

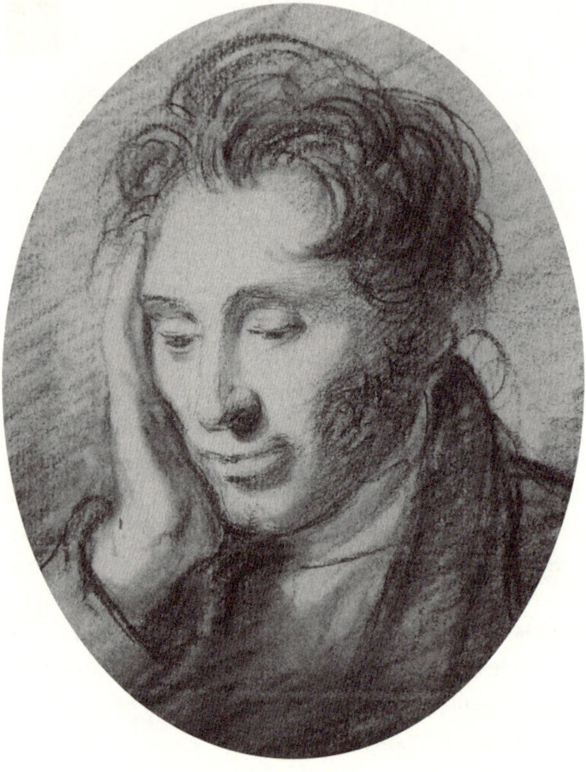

ALL THAT IS WORTH REMEMBERING

–

Selected Essays of William Hazlitt

–

with an introduction and supplementary notes by
Duncan Wu

Notting Hill Editions

Published in 2014
by Notting Hill Editions Ltd
Widworthy Barton Honiton Devon EX14 9JS

Designed by FLOK Design, Berlin, Germany
Typeset by CB editions, London

Printed and bound
by Memminger MedienCentrum, Memmingen, Germany

Introduction copyright © 2014 by Duncan Wu

Frontispiece: William Hazlitt, drawing by Sir William Allan, probably 1822, courtesy of Duncan Wu

All rights reserved

This book is sold subject to the condition that it shall not, by way of trade or otherwise, be lent, resold, hired out or otherwise circulated without the publisher's prior consent in any form of binding or cover other than that in which it is published and without a similar condition including this condition being imposed on the subsequent purchaser

A CIP record for this book
is available from the British Library

ISBN 978-1-907-90394-6

www.nottinghilleditions.com

PUBLISHER'S NOTE

The publisher would like to thank Duncan Wu for the enormous contribution he has made to this volume, and his unstinting help in its preparation.

Contents

– Introduction by Duncan Wu –

vii

– People –

xix

– Character of John Bull –

1

– On Gusto –

7

– On Good Nature –

14

– On Poetical Versatility –

23

– The *Times* Newspaper: On the Connexion Between Toad-Eaters and Tyrants –

27

– On Egotism –

42

– On Reason and Imagination –

65

– On the Spirit of Monarchy –
87

– Sir Walter Scott –
109

– The New School of Reform –
130

– London Solitude –
160

– Party Spirit –
162

Duncan Wu

– Introduction –

Why read Hazlitt today? Because no one celebrates better than he did the imaginative power of the mind as it invests itself in theatre, painting, literature, music and philosophy. But there is nothing fanciful or lightweight about him. He sees into the darkness of the human heart and perceives 'its various threads of meanness, spite, cowardice, want of feeling, and want of understanding, of indifference towards others and ignorance of ourselves'. That undeluded vision makes him as compelling as ever.

We might suppose Hazlitt the most successful failure of his period. He wanted first to be a Unitarian minister, then a great painter, then a philosopher and, finally, forced by circumstance to relinquish those aspirations, settled for life as a journalist. We are the beneficiaries of the compromises that pushed him into the pay of the *Morning Chronicle* and the most popular periodicals and magazines of his time. But he never forgot his early philosophical aspirations, and the urge to pitch an argument – whether psychological, aesthetic, or political – dominates his work. This selection from his complete prose works aims to represent that argumentative spirit at its most mature and articulate.

Almost from the first, he wrote as a genius of startling maturity. But then, for all his numerous false starts, he *was* mature – thirty-four years of age when he became a journalist, by which time he was already the author or editor of six published volumes. He was homeschooled by his father, the Reverend William Hazlitt (1737–1805), who had been educated at the University of Glasgow by (among others) Adam Smith, and passed on to his son a love of Latin and British philosophy. At the time his father was a student there, Glasgow was a remarkably enlightened institution that encouraged its students to think for themselves rather than learn by rote. The result was that many of its graduates resisted pressure to conform, preferring to worship outside the Anglican church. That explains in part why Hazlitt Sr became a Unitarian minister and wanted his son to follow him. It explains also why the future essayist failed to do so: the tradition of enquiry that drove Glasgow graduates to Socinianism nudged many at the Hackney New College, where young Hazlitt was sent to train, into atheism. It is important to add, however, that the essayist was not an atheist in the modern sense – there is no nihilism or despair in him, as in some twentieth-century writers – and there was nothing self-regarding about his refusal to believe. If he lacked faith in a benevolent Deity, he was confident that human beings possessed the power to choose the path of good over evil.

Yet these are the writings of a man whose youthful ambition would never have been to write for newspapers. When he realized he was not to be a minister he thought of cultivating his talents as an artist. That period in his life was one of its most intense. Commissioned to copy some of the great paintings in the Louvre during the brief intermission provided by the Treaty of Amiens in the midst of the lengthy conflict between Britain and France that ran from 1793 to 1815, Hazlitt was elated: 'It was *un beau jour* to me. I marched delighted through a quarter of a mile of the proudest efforts of the mind of man, a whole creation of genius, a universe of art!' To gaze today at his paintings is to bear witness to the talents of a remarkably gifted painter – but his love of Titian inspired dark, brooding, melancholy portrayals of his sitters, which did not flatter them. One portrait was returned with 'an abusive letter' while another was described as 'a good caricature likeness but a coarse painting'. Wordsworth burnt his, and joked that Hazlitt's portrait of Coleridge was 'not producible for fear of fatal consequences to married women'.

Were it not for the need to earn a salary – a contingency forced on him by a wife and young child – Hazlitt would never have turned to journalism. Painting commissions had dried up; he was writing begging letters to his friends; his wife had taken their infant child to her brother's where at least they would be made comfortable, and had probably told him their marriage was in trouble. Thanks to the lobbying of friends, he was offered a salaried post as parliamentary reporter at one of the most important daily newspapers in London, the *Morning Chronicle*. And he never looked back. He began transcribing debates in the Commons before turning to editorial commentaries on politicians of the day.

Hazlitt did not invent the essay as a literary form, but did renovate it as the vehicle later used by Virginia Woolf, George Orwell and Clive James, all of whom acknowledge his influence. He admired Montaigne (1533–92), who he described as 'a most magnanimous and undisguised egotist', and was an avid reader of Addison and Steele, authors of *The Spectator* and *The Tatler* in the early eighteenth century. 'The English journalist', Hazlitt once said, 'good-naturedly lets you into the secret both of his own affairs and those of his neighbours.' That disinterested objective was what he wanted for his own writing, and it is discernible also in that of those with whom he is associated – especially Charles Lamb.

Before Hazlitt, newspapers were dry, lifeless documents: sports reporting was rudimentary, with little indication of what actually happened, while political articles were crudely partisan. Hazlitt was ideally suited to journalism because he was capable of assessing with an unbiased and appreciative eye even those with whom he disagreed. He created the political sketch and sports commentary as we know them, and turned reviewing into a fine art. At first his innovations shocked colleagues. Alarmed by his outspokenness, James Perry, his editor at the *Chronicle*, was moved to

— *Introduction* —

apologise in print for his rough handling of Sir Thomas Lawrence, portraitist of the rich and famous. It would take more adventurous editors to allow him the liberty his genius demanded.

Nine of the essays in this book first appeared in newspapers or periodicals, three in book form. Hazlitt's collected writings run to 21 volumes, and an additional two volumes of uncollected writings were issued in 2007 – an astonishing achievement for a man who began writing professionally in his mid-thirties and died at the age of fifty-two. How did he do it? Though he had no love of writing he took tremendous pride in his ability to do it better than anyone else. In fact, he could draft a brilliant, witty, and perceptive sentence with almost no revision, as his surviving manuscripts attest.

There are many pleasures in reading Hazlitt, but the most obvious is his candour: he was the archetypal 'plain speaker'. In this selection, he expresses dislike of racism, stupidity, and the institution of the monarchy, just as he makes clear his respect for the Scotch novels and Napoleon. Authenticity of feeling comes often in the form of resistance: it was in a spirit of detached, almost scientific curiosity he analysed politicians of the day, Sir Walter Scott, and the king. He had reason to detest them but regarded them disinterestedly, revolving them in his imagination until their inner workings were exposed. There is no hypocrisy or superiority about this; he knew he had befouled his professional standing by the havoc wrought in his private life – infatuation with a much younger woman, divorce, a failed second marriage, and bankruptcy. He writes as a man who has embraced failure and so looks at the world with compassion, regardless of his subject: 'Whatever interests, is interesting' (p.50).

Our pleasure in reading Hazlitt is due in part to his ability to engage. He understands what flawed creatures we are and how desperately we aspire to be something better. Like his erstwhile mentors, Wordsworth and Coleridge, he knows that such aspirations live most intensely in the recognition of our shared humanity:

It is in vain to tell me that what excites the heart-felt sigh of youth, the tears of delight in age, and fills up the busy interval between with pleasing and lofty thoughts, is frivolous, or a waste of time, or of no use. You only by that give me a mean opinion of your ideas of utility. (p.51)

Utility: that most blinkered of doctrines. It is hard now to describe the grip on the liberal imagination which Utilitarianism exerted in Hazlitt's day. To many, including his friends, it appeared the only alternative to the conservatism that then dominated British politics. Yet he did not hesitate to condemn the manner in which Benthamite thought 'first reduces every thing to pleasure and pain, and then tramples upon and crushes these by its own sovereign will' (p.149).

Several of these essays being preoccupied explicitly with politics, it is worth reminding ourselves of the ideo-

— *Introduction* —

logical climate in which Hazlitt lived. Some critics write about him and his contemporaries as if they shared our assumptions and beliefs; nothing could be more misleading. Hazlitt spent his life in a society controlled by a small oligarchy of wealthy landowners whose principal desire was to prevent anyone else taking power. A mere 250,000 people out of 15 million had the vote (1.7 per cent of the population), including those eligible in the constituencies of Old Sarum (a depopulated mound of scorched earth on Salisbury Plain) and Dunwich (which was underwater). Manchester, Birmingham, Sheffield and Leeds, the largest industrial centres in Britain, had no representation at all. In Edinburgh and Glasgow only magistrates could vote; in Bodmin, only members of the local corporation could vote; in the constituency of Westminster, anyone could vote whose rent was more than ten pounds a year. Graduates of Oxford and Cambridge Universities had the right to vote both in their home constituency and their university constituency. Votes were always for sale.

How such a blatantly unrepresentative system commanded the respect of anyone may seem beyond us. But the fact is that, by and large, the British constitution was the envy of the world. And for most of Hazlitt's lifetime it was viewed with pride by the majority of those disenfranchised by it. There were spasmodic attempts to lobby for its reform, usually in the form of extraparliamentary campaigns mounted by small groups of working- or middle-class people, but they were suppressed with unstinting ruthlessness by the government and in any case their aims were, by our standards, modest. No one argued for universal suffrage, the idea of giving women the vote being inconceivable (though they were allowed to write political pamphlets, canvass, and act as patrons of constituencies), and very few advocated even manhood suffrage. 'Democracy' was a dirty word, associated with mob-rule and the guillotine; it was certainly not the objective of those who pushed through the Reform Act of 1832, which continued to tie the franchise to property.

Foreign though it seems to us, that was the political environment in which Hazlitt lived, and it informs every essay in this volume. When in 'On the Connexion between Toad-Eaters and Tyrants' he condemned those who prostituted their pens 'to the mock-heroic defence of the most bare-faced of all mummeries, the pretended alliance of kings and people!' (p.31), he took a risk: those writers-turned-whores were his former friends, Southey, Coleridge and Wordsworth, and they had the ear of those in power. Southey and Coleridge did not hesitate to write to the Prime Minister, Lord Liverpool, demanding that journalists like Hazlitt be imprisoned.

That did not discourage him from quizzing more exalted icons. In his day the king could declare wars, form governments, and raise armies, and his consent was indispensable if Parliament was to formulate and implement legislation. That made calling him 'mad-

— *Introduction* —

man' or 'ideot' (p.96) a more serious matter than it is today; indeed, laws were framed making it a punishable offence to print whatever the courts deemed seditious or treasonable. No wonder Thomas Paine and William Cobbett preferred to go into exile than be incarcerated like such agitators as Henry 'Orator' Hunt. It is one of the marvels of the Romantic period that Hazlitt evaded prosecution when he was so forthright – but then, this is the man who admonished his son, 'Do not gratify the enemies of liberty by putting yourself at their mercy'.

Hazlitt is one of that select group of writers who, though rooted in a specific context, transcend their historical moment: his portrait of John Bull explains the English character in the age of UKIP while his analysis of gusto reveals why some paintings move us and others leave us untouched. According to him, mankind 'is naturally a worshipper of idols and a lover of kings' (p.35) – and he can explain why. It would be a mistake, however, to read him as a bundle of miscellaneous and ramshackle opinions that have remained, through some mysterious accident, relevant. He is more than that, for his writings, disparate as they may appear, are predicated on a thesis – not something that can be claimed of all essayists.

He had begun to formulate his philosophical theory as a student at the Unitarian academy for ministers in Hackney in the 1790s. He argued that the future is distinct from the past and present because it is only there we have any chance of affecting the course of events. We are, in other words, moral agents only as we anticipate what is to come. Hazlitt's masterstroke was to posit that, in conceiving of our prospective selves, we undertake an imaginative act of sympathy identical to that by which we conceive of others. It was proof, he argued, that 'the human mind is naturally disinterested, or that it is naturally interested in the welfare of others in the same way, and from the same direct motives, by which we are impelled to the pursuit of our own interest.' It confirmed people had the ability to make choices and to act, by sheer will, in the interests of others. His point was that the choice exists, and that we are not *compelled* to act selfishly, as some philosophers claimed. He was always to call this a 'metaphysical discovery' but modern readers will recognize it as a psychological one, and in the last twenty years it has won the applause of scientists and philosophers. It provided the intellectual foundation to every essay he ever wrote.

His philosophical expertise is not why most of us read him. We return compulsively to his writings because they balance an attentiveness to the practicalities of human life with an openness to the things that make it worth living:

I hear the sound of village bells – it 'opens all the cells where memory slept' – I see a well-known prospect, my eyes are dim with manifold recollections. What say you? Am I only as a

— *Introduction* —

rational being to hear the sound, to see the object with my bodily sense? Is all the rest to be dissolved as an empty delusion, by the potent spell of unsparing philosophy? (pp.157–8)

Hazlitt's answer to this last question (lest we are in doubt) is a resounding 'No!' We love Hazlitt because he rejects the idea man is 'a savage, an automaton, or a Political Economist'. He has no patience for a purely materialist view. He is a friend to the idealizing and perfecting faculty of the imagination, a believer in the faith that places 'the heart in the centre of my moral system' (p.157). That faith was learned from Wordsworth and assured him he was a poet as much as thinker, capable of exploiting the lyricism of the language like no one else. Though racked by the illness that was to kill him, he remained capable of the inspired effusion of 'London Solitude' which evokes as persuasively now as in 1830 the experience of walking through the streets of our capital city:

And there shall pass him in his walks poets that musically sing of human feeling, priests that preach the religion of mercy, the wealthy who pity the sorrows of the poor, the sentimental whose hearts are touched by the tale of woe – and none of these shall heed him; and he may retire at night to his bedless garret, and sit cold and hungry by his empty grate; the world may be busy and cheerful and noisy around him, but no sympathy shall reach him; his heart shall be dry as Gideon's fleece while the softening dews of humanity are falling around him. (p.161)

'London Solitude' is not, ultimately, sombre or unconsoled. The image with which it concludes – the softening dews of humanity – is one of purgation. And when the time came for Hazlitt to take his leave of the world in which he lived so intensely, he was not alone. He had at his bedside his son and a small group of friends, including his colleague Charles Lamb.

There was a time, not long ago, when academic fashion forsook Hazlitt in favour of other writers; that tide has long turned. This thoughtful selection for the twenty-first century makes Hazlitt's best writings available to the general reader afresh, in a form uncluttered by notes other than those by Hazlitt himself. It is the ideal introduction to a writer whose prose is as illuminating and wise as ever, and to whom Michael Foot once paid tribute in terms of unmatched eloquence:

No man ever treasured his youth more joyously than Hazlitt did; no man ever honoured his father better; no man ever discharged with such good faith the debts of honour he owed to the favourite authors of his youth – Burke, Rousseau, Cervantes, Montaigne and a legion more. No critic (except perhaps a few fellow poets, and not many of them) ever heard the strange language of a new school of poetry with such an alert sympathy, and certainly no critic ever welcomed the innovation with greater daring and, despite all subsequent political feuds, with more persistence and warmth.

Georgetown University
30 July 2014

– People –

Arkwright, Sir Richard (1732–92), industrialist and inventor
of the spinning jenny.
Bentham, Jeremy (1748–1832), Utilitarian philosopher
criticized by Hazlitt for overweening rationalism and
cold-bloodedness; he was also Hazlitt's landlord.
Blackwood, William (1776–1834), publisher of *Blackwood's
Edinburgh Magazine*, which made Hazlitt one of its *bêtes
noires*. Hazlitt sued Blackwood for damages in 1818,
and the case was settled out of court.
Buckingham, James Silk (1786–1855), established at Calcutta
in 1818 a paper called *The Calcutta Journal*, which
exposed the abuses of the Indian government, and was
suppressed in April 1823.
'Burke': Edmund Burke (1729–97), Whig politician and
author of one of Hazlitt's favourite books, *Reflections on
the Revolution in France* (1790) – though he loathed its
anti-revolutionary stance.
Canning, George (1770–1827), Irish-born British statesman,
remembered for his liberal policies as Foreign Secretary
from 1822 to 1827.
'Castlereagh': Robert Stewart, Viscount Castlereagh and
second Marquess of Londonderry (1769–1822),
politician, had been complicit in the ruthless
suppression of the United Irishmen in 1798, and
orchestrated the Congress at Vienna that reinstated the
Bourbon monarchy after Napoleon's defeat.

Catalani, Angelica (1780–1849), Italian soprano, one of the most successful opera singers of her day.

Coleridge, Samuel Taylor (1772–1834), journalist and poet, encouraged Hazlitt as a young man and disappointed him in later years for the conservative views expressed in the two *Lay Sermons* (1816–17) and *Aids to Reflection* (1825).

Constable, Archibald (1774–1827), publisher of Hazlitt's *The Round Table* (1817), rival and enemy of William Blackwood.

Croker, John Wilson (1780–1857), Irish-born essayist and critic, whose regressive taste and conservative politics made him hostile to Keats and Hazlitt, among many others.

Dignum, Charles (1765–1827), tenor singer, who Hazlitt saw on his first visit to the theatre in 1790.

'Miss Edgeworth': Maria Edgeworth (1768–1849), novelist and educationalist, author of *Castle Rackrent* (1800).

'Eldon': John Scott, first earl of Eldon (1751–1838), lord chancellor, memorable for his repressive policy towards internal dissent and opposition to Catholic emancipation.

Erskine, Thomas, first Baron Erskine (1750–1823), British lawyer, fondly remembered by Hazlitt as a distinguished advocate for liberty and enlightened Lord Chancellor.

'Ferdinand': Ferdinand VII (1784–1833) was King of Spain twice – in 1808, and again from 1813 to 1833. He was an absolutist tyrant and reinstated the Spanish Inquisition in the form of 'Faith Commissions'.

'Fox': Charles James Fox (1749–1806), leader of the whig party in Parliament. Hazlitt says he died at the house of Lord Holland but in fact he died at Chiswick House in west London.

Goldsmith, Oliver (1728–74), poet, novelist and playwright,

— *People* —

was a friend of Johnson and Reynolds.

Hall, Joseph (1764–1831), celebrated Baptist preacher, announced his removal from Leicester to Bristol in February 1826.

Hobhouse, John Cam, Baron Broughton (1786–1869), statesman, friend of Lord Byron. He contested the seat at Westminster as an independent radical in 1819, when Hazlitt voted for him. His defeat was due to the intervention of Francis Place, associate of Bentham, who launched a ferocious attack on the whigs.

'Holland': Henry Richard Fox (later Vassall), third Baron Holland of Holland and third Baron Holland of Foxley (1773–1840), politician and man of letters, was nephew of Charles James Fox, the leader of the whigs.

Kaufmann, Maria Anna Angelica (1741–1807), historical and portrait painter, born in Switzerland, made her name in London from 1766 onwards.

Kean, Edmund (1787–1833), the most innovatory stage actor of his generation, heralded an acting style close to the one that prevails today. Hazlitt was present when he first erupted onto the London stage as Shylock, and his reviews are the best surviving record of what Kean's performances were like.

'king': George III (1738–1820); the Regency Act of February 1811 conferred power on his eldest son who succeeded to the throne as George IV in 1820 (1762–1830).

'Lord Chancellor', see Eldon.

Louis XVIII (1755–1824), Bourbon monarch reinstated to the French throne by the terms of the Congress of Vienna, who ruled France from 1814 to 1824.

Mandeville, Bernard (bap.1670, died 1733), author of one of Hazlitt's favourite books of philosophy, *The Fable of the Bees* (1714).

Mill, James (1773–1836), British historian, economist, and philosopher, was a disciple of Bentham.

'Naimbanna': John Frederick Nemgbana, or Naimbana (1768–93), son of Nemgbana, regent of the Koya Temne in Sierra Leone, was educated in England. He returned home with the intention of converting his people to Christianity but died shortly after arrival at Freetown.

Owen, Robert (1771–1858), industrialist, practiced an early form of socialism at his mill at New Lanark, described in his *New View of Society* (1813–14).

Paine, Thomas (1737–1809), was one of Hazlitt's heroes – the republican best known for *The Rights of Man* (1791–2), for which he went into exile.

Paley, William (1743–1805), theologian and philosopher, whose lectures on ethics, *The Principles of Moral and Political Philosophy* (1785) were indebted to Abraham Tucker's *The Light of Nature Pursued* (7 vols., 1768–78).

Peacock, Thomas Love (1785–1866), novelist, was appointed in 1819, at the same time as James Mill, to the India House; he was associated with the Utilitarians. His *Rhododaphne* was published in 1818.

Peel, Sir Robert, second baronet (1788–1850), became Home Secretary in 1822 and immediately set about the measures that culminated in the founding of the Metropolitan Police Force in 1829.

Place, Francis (1771–1854), English radical reformer, associate of Jeremy Bentham, and successful tailor. Hazlitt never forgave Place for having prevented the election of Hobhouse as an independent radical in his constituency of Westminster in 1819.

Potato, Talking, see Croker.

Reynolds, Sir Joshua (1723–92), the most successful portrait

— *People* —

painter of his time, was tutor to Hazlitt's brother John, also a painter. Hazlitt studied Reynolds's *Discourses* closely and often refers to them.

Romanzini, Maria Theresa (1769–1838), mezzo-soprano who enjoyed a successful theatrical career until her final stage appearance in 1822.

Scott, John (1784–1821), journalist, was a colleague of Hazlitt's. He died after being fatally wounded in a duel by Jonathan Christie, a close associate of Walter Scott (no relation).

Scott, Sir Walter (1771–1832). To Hazlitt, the author of the *Waverley* novels was a 'sly old knave' who he had the chance to meet on at least two occasions; he declined to do so because he detested Scott's loyalty to the forces of conservatism.

Sheridan, Richard Brinsley (1751–1816), playwright and politician, the companion of Fox and Burke.

Suett, Richard (1755–1805), comedian and singer, was much admired by Hazlitt.

'*The Times*', editor of: John Stoddart (1773–1856), Hazlitt's brother-in-law, was a leader writer at *The Times* and as editor swung the paper sharply to the right, so much as to alarm its proprietor, John Walter the second, who sacked him at the end of 1816.

Tucker, Abraham (1705–1774), was author of a book of philosophy, *The Light of Nature Pursued* (7 vols., 1768–78), which Hazlitt abridged and published in a one-volume edition in 1807.

Vansittart, Nicholas, first Baron Bexley (1766–1851), Tory politician who as Chancellor of the Exchequer from 1812 to 1822 presided over recession, rising unemployment, and increasing local taxation, and was regarded as a failure even by those of his own party.

Westall, Richard (1765–1836), historical painter, made RA in 1794.

Wordsworth, William (1770–1850), poet, first met Hazlitt in 1798 while meditating a revolutionary poem, 'The Recluse'. Hazlitt never forgave him for accepting the patronage of aristocrats and celebrating Waterloo in a poem that declared Carnage the daughter of God.

Young, Charles Mayne (1777–1856) was one of the leading tragedians of his day, challenged only by Kean.

– Character of John Bull –

First published *Examiner*, 19 May 1816; reproduced from *The Round Table* (1817). Few essays demonstrate so vividly Hazlitt's ability to view the English from the perspective of an outsider. His father being an Irishman with connections to the rebels of 1798 and 1803, Hazlitt was sensitive to the casual brutalities of the English. 'On the Spirit of Monarchy' and 'Party Spirit' extend some of the arguments presented here.

In a late number of a respectable publication, there is the following description of the French character:—

'Extremes meet. This is the only way of accounting for that enigma, the French character. It has often been remarked, that this ingenious nation exhibits more striking contradictions than any other that ever existed. They are the gayest of the gay, and the gravest of the grave. Their very faces pass at once from an expression of the most lively animation, when they are in conversation or in action, to a melancholy blank. They are the lightest and most volatile, and, at the same time, the most plodding, mechanical, and laborious people in Europe. They are one moment the slaves of the most contemptible prejudices, and the next launch out into all the extravagance of the most abstract speculations. In matters of taste they are as inexorable as they are lax in questions of morality: they judge of the one by rules, of the other by their inclinations. It seems at times as if nothing could shock them, and yet they are offended at the merest trifles. The smallest things make the greatest impression on them. From the facility with which they can accommodate themselves to circumstances, they have no fixed principles or real character. They are always that which gives them least pain, or costs them least trouble. They easily disentangle their thoughts from whatever causes the slightest uneasiness, and direct their sensibility to flow in any channels they think proper. Their whole existence is more theatrical than real—their sentiments put on or off like the dress of an actor. Words are with them equivalent to things. They say what is agreeable, and believe what they say. Virtue and vice, good and evil, liberty and slavery, are matters almost of indifference. Their natural self-complacency stands them in stead of all other advantages.'

The foregoing account is pretty near the truth; we have nothing to say against it; but we shall here endeavour to do a like piece of justice to our countrymen, who are too apt to mistake the vices of others for so many virtues in themselves.

If a Frenchman is pleased with every thing, John Bull is pleased with nothing, and that is a fault. He is, to be sure, fond of having his own way, till you let him have it. He is a very headstrong animal, who mistakes

— *Character of John Bull* —

the spirit of contradiction for the love of independence, and proves himself to be in the right by the obstinacy with which he stickles for the wrong. You cannot put him so much out of his way, as by agreeing with him. He is never in such good humour as with what gives him the spleen, and is most satisfied when he is sulky. If you find fault with him, he is in a rage; and if you praise him, suspects you have a design upon him. He recommends himself to another by affronting him, and if that will not do, knocks him down to convince him of his sincerity. He gives himself such airs as no mortal ever did, and wonders at the rest of the world for not thinking him the most amiable person breathing. John means well too, but he has an odd way of shewing it, by a total disregard of other people's feelings and opinions. He is sincere, for he tells you at the first word he does not like you; and never deceives, for he never offers to serve you. A civil answer is too much to expect from him. A word costs him more than a blow. He is silent because he has nothing to say, and he looks stupid because he is so. He has the strangest notions of beauty. The expression he values most in the human countenance is an appearance of roast beef and plum-pudding; and if he has a red face and round belly, thinks himself a great man. He is a little purse-proud, and has a better opinion of himself for having made a full meal. But his greatest delight is in a bugbear. This he must have, be the consequence what it may. Whoever will give him that, may lead him by the nose, and pick his pocket at the same time. An idiot in a country town, a Presbyterian parson, a dog with a cannister tied to his tail, a bull-bait, or a fox-hunt, are irresistible attractions to him. The Pope was formerly his great aversion, and latterly, a cap of liberty is a thing he cannot abide. He discarded the Pope, and defied the Inquisition, called the French a nation of slaves and beggars, and abused their *Grand Monarque* for a tyrant, cut off one king's head, and exiled another, set up a Dutch Stadtholder, and elected a Hanoverian Elector to be king over him, to shew he would have his own way, and to teach the rest of the world what they should do: but since other people took to imitating his example, John has taken it into his head to hinder them, will have a monopoly of rebellion and regicide to himself, has become sworn brother to the Pope, and stands by the Inquisition, restores his old enemies the Bourbons, and reads *a great moral lesson* to their subjects, persuades himself that the Dutch Stadtholder and the Hanoverian Elector came to reign over him by divine right, and does all he can to prove himself a beast to make other people slaves. The truth is, John was always a surly, meddlesome, obstinate fellow, and of late years his *head* has not been quite right!—In short, John is a great blockhead and a great bully, and requires (what he has been long labouring for) a hundred years of slavery to bring him to his senses. He will have it that he is a great patriot, for he hates all other countries; that he is wise, for he thinks all other people fools; that he is honest, for he calls all other people whores and rogues. If being in an ill-humour all one's life is the perfection of human nature, then John is very near it. He beats his wife, quarrels with his neighbours, damns his servants, and gets drunk to kill the time and keep up his spirits, and firmly believes himself the only unexceptionable, accomplished, moral and religious character in Christendom. He boasts of the excellence of the laws, and the goodness of his own disposition; and yet there are more people hanged in England than in all Europe besides: he boasts of the modesty of his countrywomen, and yet there are more prostitutes in the streets of London than in all the capitals of Europe put together. He piques himself on his comforts, because he is the most uncomfortable of mortals; and because he has no enjoyment in society, seeks it, as he says, at his fireside,—where he may be stupid as a matter of course, sullen as a matter of right, and as ridiculous as he chooses without being laughed at. His liberty is the effect of his self-will; his religion owing to the spleen; his temper to the climate. He is an industrious animal, because he has no taste for amusement, and had rather work six days in the week than be idle one. His awkward attempts at gaiety are the jest of other nations. 'They,' (the English,) says Froissard, speaking of the meeting of the Black Prince and the French King, 'amused themselves sadly, according to the custom of their country,'—*se re-jouissoient tristement, selon la coutume de leur pays.* Their patience of

— ALL THAT IS WORTH REMEMBERING —

labour is confined to what is repugnant and disagreeable in itself, to the drudgery of the mechanic arts, and does not extend to the fine arts; that is, they are indifferent to pain, but insensible to pleasure. They will stand in a trench, or march up to a breach, but they cannot bear to dwell long on an agreeable object. They can no more submit to regularity in art than to decency in behaviour. Their pictures are as coarse and slovenly as their address.—John boasts of his great men, without much right to do so; not that he has not had them, but because he neither knows nor cares any thing about them but to swagger over other nations. That which chiefly hits John's fancy in Shakspeare is that he was a deer-stealer in his youth; and, as for Newton's discoveries, he hardly knows to this day that the earth is round. John's oaths, which are quite characteristic, have got him the nickname of *Monsieur God damn me.* They are profane, a Frenchman's indecent. One swears by his vices, the other by their punishment. After all John's blustering, he is but a dolt. His habitual jealousy of others makes him the inevitable dupe of quacks and impostors of all sorts; he goes all lengths with one party out of spite to another; his zeal is as furious as his antipathies are unfounded; and there is nothing half so absurd or ignorant of its own intentions as an English mob.

– On Gusto –

First published *Examiner*, 26 May 1816; reproduced from *The Round Table* (1817). This is Hazlitt's most important essay on aesthetics. It looks back to Wordsworth's note to 'The Thorn' (*Lyrical Ballads*, 1800), which stated that 'poetry is passion; it is the history or science of feelings'. Hazlitt develops Wordsworth's idea in his own, original way, finding his most telling illustration in the paintings of Titian, whose 'heads seem to think – his bodies seem to feel'. His point is that the artist's job is to transcend the self so as completely to apprehend the sensations of another being or object. This idea would influence Keats's concept of 'negative capability'.

Gusto in art is power or passion defining any object.—It is not so difficult to explain this term in what relates to expression (of which it may be said to be the highest degree) as in what relates to things without expression, to the natural appearances of objects, as mere colour or form. In one sense, however, there is hardly any object entirely devoid of expression, without some character of power belonging to it, some precise association with pleasure or pain: and it is in giving this truth of character from the truth of feeling, whether in the highest or the lowest degree, but always in the highest degree of which the subject is capable, that gusto consists.

There is a gusto in the colouring of Titian. Not only do his heads seem to think—his bodies seem to feel. This is what the Italians mean by the *morbidezza* of his flesh-colour. It seems sensitive and alive all over; not merely to have the look and texture of flesh, but the feeling in itself. For example, the limbs of his female figures have a luxurious softness and delicacy, which appears conscious of the pleasure of the beholder. As the objects themselves in nature would produce an impression on the sense, distinct from every other object, and having something divine in it, which the heart owns and the imagination consecrates, the objects in the picture preserve the same impression, absolute, unimpaired, stamped with all the truth of passion, the pride of the eye, and the charm of beauty. Rubens makes his flesh-colour like flowers; Albano's is like ivory; Titian's is like flesh, and like nothing else. It is as different from that of other painters, as the skin is from a piece of white or red drapery thrown over it. The blood circulates here and there, the blue veins just appear, the rest is distinguished throughout only by that sort of tingling sensation to the eye, which the body feels within itself. This is gusto.—Vandyke's flesh-colour, though it has great truth and purity, wants gusto. It has not the internal character, the living principle in it. It is a smooth surface, not a warm, moving mass. It is painted without passion, with indifference.

— *On Gusto* —

The hand only has been concerned. The impression slides off from the eye, and does not, like the tones of Titian's pencil, leave a sting behind it in the mind of the spectator. The eye does not acquire a taste or appetite for what it sees. In a word, gusto in painting is where the impression made on one sense excites by affinity those of another.

Michael Angelo's forms are full of gusto. They every where obtrude the sense of power upon the eye. His limbs convey an idea of muscular strength, of moral grandeur, and even of intellectual dignity: they are firm, commanding, broad, and massy, capable of executing with ease the determined purposes of the will. His faces have no other expression than his figures, conscious power and capacity. They appear only to think what they shall do, and to know that they can do it. This is what is meant by saying that his style is hard and masculine. It is the reverse of Correggio's, which is effeminate. That is, the gusto of Michael Angelo consists in expressing energy of will without proportionable sensibility, Correggio's in expressing exquisite sensibility without energy of will. In Correggio's faces as well as figures we see neither bones nor muscles, but then what a soul is there, full of sweetness and of grace—pure, playful, soft, angelical! There is sentiment enough in a hand painted by Correggio to set up a school of history painters. Whenever we look at the hands of Correggio's women or of Raphael's, we always wish to touch them.

Again, Titian's landscapes have a prodigious gusto, both in the colouring and forms. We shall never forget one that we saw many years ago in the Orleans Gallery of Actaeon hunting. It had a brown, mellow, autumnal look. The sky was of the colour of stone. The winds seemed to sing through the rustling branches of the trees, and already you might hear the twanging of bows resound through the tangled mazes of the wood. Mr West, we understand, has this landscape. He will know if this description of it is just. The landscape background of the St Peter Martyr is another well known instance of the power of this great painter to give a romantic interest and an appropriate character to the objects of his pencil, where every circumstance adds to the effect of the scene,—the bold trunks of the tall forest trees, the trailing ground plants, with that cold convent spire rising in the distance, amidst the blue sapphire mountains and the golden sky.

Rubens has a great deal of gusto in his Fauns and Satyrs, and in all that expresses motion, but in nothing else. Rembrandt has it in every thing; every thing in his pictures has a tangible character. If he puts a diamond in the ear of a Burgomaster's wife, it is of the first water; and his furs and stuffs are proof against a Russian winter. Raphael's gusto was only in expression; he had no idea of the character of any thing but the human form. The dryness and poverty of his style in other respects is a phenomenon in the art. His trees are like sprigs of grass stuck in a book of botanical specimens.

— *On Gusto* —

Was it that Raphael never had time to go beyond the walls of Rome? That he was always in the streets, at church, or in the bath? He was not one of the Society of Arcadians.*

Claude's landscapes, perfect as they are, want gusto. This is not easy to explain. They are perfect abstractions of the visible images of things; they speak the visible language of nature truly. They resemble a mirror or a microscope. To the eye only they are more perfect than any other landscapes that ever were or will be painted; they give more of nature, as cognizable by one sense alone; but they lay an equal stress on all visible impressions; they do not interpret one sense by another; they do not distinguish the character of different objects as we are taught, and can only be taught, to distinguish them by their effect on the different senses. That is, his eye wanted imagination: it did not strongly sympathize with his other faculties. He saw the atmosphere, but he did not feel it. He painted the trunk of a tree or a rock in the foreground as smooth— with as complete an abstraction of the gross, tangible impression, as any other part of the picture; his trees

* Raphael not only could not paint a landscape; he could not paint people in a landscape. He could not have painted the heads or the figures, or even the dresses of the St Peter Martyr. His figures have always an *indoor* look, that is, a set, determined, voluntary, dramatic character, arising from their own passions, or a watchfulness of those of others, and want that wild uncertainty of expression, which is connected with the accidents of nature and the changes of the elements. He has nothing *romantic* about him.

— ALL THAT IS WORTH REMEMBERING —

are perfectly beautiful, but quite immoveable; they have a look of enchantment. In short, his landscapes are unequalled imitations of nature, released from its subjection to the elements,—as if all objects were become a delightful fairy vision, and the eye had rarefied and refined away the other senses.

The gusto in the Greek statues is of a very singular kind. The sense of perfect form nearly occupies the whole mind, and hardly suffers it to dwell on any other feeling. It seems enough for them *to be,* without acting or suffering. Their forms are ideal, spiritual. Their beauty is power. By their beauty they are raised above the frailties of pain or passion; by their beauty they are deified.

The infinite quantity of dramatic invention in Shakspeare takes from his gusto. The power he delights to shew is not intense, but discursive. He never insists on any thing as much as he might, except a quibble. Milton has great gusto. He repeats his blow twice; grapples with and exhausts his subject. His imagination has a double relish of its objects, an inveterate attachment to the things he describes, and to the words describing them.

'Or where Chineses drive
With sails and wind their *cany* waggons *light.*'
*   *   *   *   *   *   *   *   *   *   *

'Wild above rule or art, *enormous* bliss.'

— *On Gusto* —

There is a gusto in Pope's compliments, in Dryden's satires, and Prior's tales; and among prose-writers, Boccaccio and Rabelais had the most of it. We will only mention one other work which appears to us to be full of gusto, and that is the *Beggar's Opera.* If it is not, we are altogether mistaken in our notions on this delicate subject.

– On Good Nature –

First published *Examiner*, 9 June 1816; reproduced from *The Round Table* (1817). This is one of Hazlitt's most devastating political essays, its strategy being to define something usually regarded favourably as the hallmark of selfish, unjust, illiberal tyrants. In the version published in *The Examiner*, he included a few additional remarks later removed because they invited prosecution: 'Henry VIII was a good-natured monarch. He cut off his wives' heads with as little ceremony as if they had been eels. This character ought, as Mr Cobbett says, to be hooted off the stage, as a disgrace to human nature. Shakespeare represented kings as they were in his time.'

Lord Shaftesbury somewhere remarks, that a great many people pass for very good-natured persons, for no other reason than because they care about nobody but themselves; and, consequently, as nothing annoys them but what touches their own interest, they never irritate themselves unnecessarily about what does not concern them, and seem to be made of the very milk of human kindness.

Good-nature, or what is often considered as such, is the most selfish of all the virtues: it is nine times out of ten mere indolence of disposition. A good-natured

— *On Good Nature* —

man is, generally speaking, one who does not like to be put out of his way; and as long as he can help it, that is, till the provocation comes home to himself, he will not. He does not create fictitious uneasiness out of the distresses of others; he does not fret and fume, and make himself uncomfortable about things he cannot mend, and that no way concern him, even if he could: but then there is no one who is more apt to be disconcerted by what puts him to any personal inconvenience, however trifling; who is more tenacious of his selfish indulgences, however unreasonable; or who resents more violently any interruption of his ease and comforts, the very trouble he is put to in resenting it being felt as an aggravation of the injury. A person of this character feels no emotions of anger or detestation, if you tell him of the devastation of a province, or the massacre of the inhabitants of a town, or the enslaving of a people; but if his dinner is spoiled by a lump of soot falling down the chimney, he is thrown into the utmost confusion, and can hardly recover a decent command of his temper for the whole day. He thinks nothing can go amiss, so long as he is at his ease, though a pain in his little finger makes him so peevish and quarrelsome, that nobody can come near him. Knavery and injustice in the abstract are things that by no means ruffle his temper, or alter the serenity of his countenance, unless he is to be the sufferer by them; nor is he ever betrayed into a passion in answering a sophism, if he does not think it immediately directed against his own interest.

— ALL THAT IS WORTH REMEMBERING —

On the contrary, we sometimes meet with persons who regularly heat themselves in an argument, and get out of humour on every occasion, and make themselves obnoxious to a whole company about nothing. This is not because they are ill-tempered, but because they are in earnest. Good-nature is a hypocrite: it tries to pass off its love of its own ease and indifference to every thing else for a particular softness and mildness of disposition. All people get in a passion, and lose their temper, if you offer to strike them, or cheat them of their money, that is, if you interfere with that which they are really interested in. Tread on the heel of one of these good-natured persons, who do not care if the whole world is in flames, and see how he will bear it. If the truth were known, the most disagreeable people are the most amiable. They are the only persons who feel an interest in what does not concern them. They have as much regard for others as they have for themselves. They have as many vexations and causes of complaint as there are in the world. They are general righters of wrongs, and redressers of grievances. They not only are annoyed by what they can help, by an act of inhumanity done in the next street, or in a neighbouring country by their own countrymen, they not only do not claim any share in the glory, and hate it the more, the more brilliant the success,—but a piece of injustice done three thousand years ago touches them to the quick. They have an unfortunate attachment to a set of abstract phrases, such as *liberty*, *truth*, *justice*, *humanity*, *honour*, which

— *On Good Nature* —

are continually abused by knaves, and misunderstood by fools, and they can hardly contain themselves for spleen. They have something to keep them in perpetual hot-water. No sooner is one question set at rest than another rises up to perplex them. They wear themselves to the bone in the affairs of other people, to whom they can do no manner of service, to the neglect of their own business and pleasure. They tease themselves to death about the morality of the Turks, or the politics of the French. There are certain words that afflict their ears, and things that lacerate their souls, and remain a plague-spot there forever after. They have a fellow-feeling with all that has been done, said, or thought in the world. They have an interest in all science and in all art. They hate a lie as much as a wrong, for truth is the foundation of all justice. Truth is the first thing in their thoughts, then mankind, then their country, last themselves. They love excellence, and bow to fame, which is the shadow of it. Above all, they are anxious to see justice done to the dead, as the best encouragement to the living, and the lasting inheritance of future generations. They do not like to see a great principle undermined, or the fall of a great man. They would sooner forgive a blow in the face than a wanton attack on acknowledged reputation. The contempt in which the French hold Shakspeare is a serious evil to them; nor do they think the matter mended, when they hear an Englishman, who would be thought a profound one, say that Voltaire was a man without wit. They are vexed to see genius playing at Tom Fool, and honesty turned bawd. It gives them a cutting sensation to see a number of things which, as they are unpleasant to see, we shall not here repeat. In short, they have a passion for truth; they feel the same attachment to the idea of what is right, that a knave does to his interest, or that a good-natured man does to his ease; and they have as many sources of uneasiness as there are actual or supposed deviations from this standard in the sum of things, or as there is a possibility of folly and mischief in the world.

Principle is a passion for truth; an incorrigible attachment to a general proposition. Good-nature is humanity that costs nothing. No good-natured man was ever a martyr to a cause, in religion or politics. He has no idea of striving against the stream. He may become a good courtier and a loyal subject; and it is hard if he does not, for he has nothing to do in that case but to consult his ease, interest, and outward appearances. The Vicar of Bray was a good-natured man. What a pity he was but a vicar! A good-natured man is utterly unfit for any situation or office in life that requires integrity, fortitude, or generosity,—any sacrifice, except of opinion, or any exertion, but to please. A good-natured man will debauch his friend's mistress, if he has an opportunity; and betray his friend, sooner than share disgrace or danger with him. He will not forego the smallest gratification to save the whole world. He makes his own convenience the standard of right and wrong. He avoids the feeling of pain in himself, and

— *On Good Nature* —

shuts his eyes to the sufferings of others. He will put a malefactor or an innocent person (no matter which) to the rack, and only laugh at the uncouthness of the gestures, or wonder that he is so unmannerly as to cry out. There is no villany to which he will not lend a helping hand with great coolness and cordiality, for he sees only the pleasant and profitable side of things. He will assent to a falsehood with a leer of complacency, and applaud any atrocity that comes recommended in the garb of authority. He will betray his country to please a Minister, and sign the death-warrant of thousands of wretches, rather than forfeit the congenial smile, the well-known squeeze of the hand. The shrieks of death, the torture of mangled limbs, the last groans of despair, are things that shock his smooth humanity too much ever to make an impression on it: his good-nature sympathizes only with the smile, the bow, the gracious salutation, the fawning answer: vice loses its sting, and corruption its poison, in the oily gentleness of his disposition. He will not hear of any thing wrong in Church or State. He will defend every abuse by which any thing is to be got, every dirty job, every act of every Minister. In an extreme case, a very good-natured man indeed may try to hang twelve honester men than himself to rise at the Bar, and forge the seal of the realm to continue his colleagues a week longer in office. He is a slave to the will of others, a coward to their prejudices, a tool of their vices. A good-natured man is no more fit to be trusted in public affairs, than a coward or a woman is to lead an army. Spleen is the soul of patriotism and of public good. Lord Castlereagh is a good-natured man, Lord Eldon is a good-natured man, Charles Fox was a good-natured man. The last instance is the most decisive.—The definition of a true patriot is *a good hater.*

A king, who is a good-natured man, is in a fair way of being a great tyrant. A king ought to feel concern for all to whom his power extends; but a good-natured man cares only about himself. If he has a good appetite, eats and sleeps well, nothing in the universe besides can disturb him. The destruction of the lives or liberties of his subjects will not stop him in the least of his caprices, but will concoct well with his bile, and 'good digestion wait on appetite, and health on both.' He will send out his mandate to kill and destroy with the same indifference or satisfaction that he performs any natural function of his body. The consequences are placed beyond the reach of his imagination, or would not affect him if they were not, for he is a fool, and good-natured. A good-natured man hates more than any one else whatever thwarts his will, or contradicts his prejudices; and if he has the power to prevent it, depend upon it, he will use it without remorse and without control.

There is a lower species of this character which is what is usually understood by a *well-meaning man. A* well-meaning man is one who often does a great deal of mischief without any kind of malice. He means no one any harm, if it is not for his interest. He is not a knave,

— *On Good Nature* —

nor perfectly honest. He does not easily resign a good place. Mr Vansittart is a well-meaning man.

The Irish are a good-natured people; they have many virtues, but their virtues are those of the heart, not of the head. In their passions and affections they are sincere, but they are hypocrites in understanding. If they once begin to calculate the consequences, self-interest prevails. An Irishman who trusts to his principles, and a Scotchman who yields to his impulses, are equally dangerous.—The Irish have wit, genius, eloquence, imagination, affections: but they want coherence of understanding, and consequently have no standard of thought or action. Their strength of mind does not keep pace with the warmth of their feelings, or the quickness of their conceptions. Their animal spirits run away with them: their reason is a jade. There is something crude, indigested, rash, and discordant, in almost all that they do or say. They have no system, no abstract ideas. They are 'every thing by starts, and nothing long.' They are a wild people. They hate whatever imposes a law on their understandings, or a yoke on their wills. To betray the principles they are most bound by their own professions and the expectations of others to maintain, is with them a reclamation of their original rights, and to fly in the face of their benefactors and friends, an assertion of their natural freedom of will. They want consistency and good faith. They unite fierceness with levity. In the midst of their headlong impulses, they have an under-current of

— ALL THAT IS WORTH REMEMBERING —

selfishness and cunning, which in the end gets the better of them. Their feelings, when no longer excited by novelty or opposition, grow cold and stagnant. Their blood, if not heated by passion, turns to poison. They have a rancour in their hatred of any object they have abandoned, proportioned to the attachment they have professed to it. Their zeal, converted against itself, is furious. The late Mr Burke was an instance of an Irish patriot and philosopher. He abused metaphysics, because he could make nothing out of them, and turned his back upon liberty, when he found he could get nothing more by her.*—See to the same purpose the winding up of the character of Judy in Miss Edgeworth's *Castle Rackrent*.

---

* This man (Burke) who was a half poet and a half philosopher, has done more mischief than perhaps any other person in the world. His understanding was not competent to the discovery of any truth, but it was sufficient to palliate a falsehood; his reasons, of little weight in themselves, thrown into the scale of powers, were dreadful. Without genius to adorn the beautiful, he had the art to throw a dazzling veil over the deformed and disgusting; and to strew the flowers of imagination over the rotten carcase of corruption, not to prevent, but to communicate the infection. His jealousy of Rousseau was one chief cause of his opposition to the French Revolution. The writings of the one had changed the institutions of a kingdom; while the speeches of the other, with the intrigues of his whole party, had changed nothing but the *turnspit of the King's kitchen.* He would have blotted out the broad pure light of Heaven, because it did not first shine in at the little Gothic windows of St Stephen's Chapel. The genius of Rousseau had levelled the towers of the Bastile with the dust; our zealous reformist, who would rather be doing mischief than nothing, tried, therefore, to patch them up again, by calling that loathsome dungeon the King's castle, and by fulsome adulation of the virtues of a Court strumpet. This man,—but enough of him here.

– On Poetical Versatility –

First published *Examiner*, 22 December 1816; reproduced from *The Round Table* (1817). Although Hazlitt is writing of poets generally, three in particular were in his mind as he formulated this essay: Coleridge, Wordsworth and Southey, who collectively comprised one of the biggest disappointments in his life. He first met Wordsworth when he was embarked on a poem that (it was hoped) would end inequalities of class and wealth; in 1794, Coleridge and Southey planned to set up a commune in America and when he first met them they were still discussing liberal ideas. During the first two decades of the nineteenth century he watched in dismay as all three became middle-aged reactionaries: Wordsworth campaigned for Lord Lonsdale (a Tory) in 1818 ('Sad – sad – sad', was Keats's judgement); Coleridge sank his early promise in opium addiction; while Southey accepted the post of Poet Laureate and wrote lengthy articles on the viciousness of the working-class. Hazlitt's response is to condemn their susceptibility to the blandishments of the rich and powerful.

T he spirit of poetry is in itself favourable to humanity and liberty: but, we suspect, not when its aid is most wanted. The spirit of poetry is not the spirit of mortification or of martyrdom. Poetry dwells in a perpetual Utopia of its own, and is, for that reason, very ill calculated to make a Paradise upon earth, by encountering the shocks and disappointments of the world. Poetry, like law, is a fiction; only a more agreeable one. It does not create difficulties where they do not exist; but contrives to get rid of them, whether they exist or not. It is not entangled in cobwebs of its own making, but soars above all obstacles. It cannot be 'constrained by mastery.' It has the range of the universe; it traverses the empyreum, and looks down on nature from a higher sphere. When it lights upon the earth, it loses some of its dignity and its use. Its strength is in its wings; its element the air. Standing on its feet, jostling with the crowd, it is liable to be overthrown, trampled on, and defaced; for its wings are of a dazzling brightness, 'heavens own tinct,' and the least soil upon them shews to disadvantage. Sullied, degraded as we have seen it, we shall not insult over it, but leave it to Time to take out the stains, seeing it is a thing immortal as itself. 'Being so majestical, we should do it wrong to offer it the shew of violence.' But the best things, in their abuse, often become the worst; and so it is with poetry, when it is diverted from its proper end. Poets live in an ideal world, where they make every thing out according to their wishes and fancies. They either find things delightful, or make them so. They feign the beautiful and grand out of their own minds, and imagine all things to be, not what they are, but what they

— *On Poetical Versatility* —

ought to be. They are naturally inventors, creators of truth, of love, and beauty: and while they speak to us from the sacred shrine of their own hearts, while they pour out the pure treasures of thought to the world, they cannot be too much admired and applauded: but when, forgetting their high calling, and becoming tools and puppets in the hands of power, they would pass off the gewgaws of corruption and love-tokens of self interest as the gifts of the Muse, they cannot be too much despised and shunned. We do not like novels founded on facts, nor do we like poets turned courtiers. Poets, it has been said, succeed best in fiction: and they should for the most part stick to it. Invention, not upon an imaginary subject, is a lie: the varnishing over the vices or deformity of actual objects is hypocrisy. Players leave their finery at the stage-door, or they would be hooted; poets come out into the world with all their bravery on, and yet they would pass for *bona fide* persons. They lend the colours of fancy to whatever they see: whatever they touch becomes gold, though it were lead. With them every Joan is a lady; and kings and queens are human. Matters of fact they embellish at their will, and reason is the plaything of their passions, their caprice, or interest. There is no practice so base of which they will not become the panders: no sophistry of which their understanding may not be made the voluntary dupe. Their only object is to please their fancy. Their souls are effeminate, half man and half woman:—they want fortitude, and are without principle. If things do not turn out according to their wishes, they will make their wishes turn round to things. They can easily overlook whatever they do not like, and make an idol of any thing they please. The object of poetry is to please: this art naturally gives pleasure, and excites admiration. Poets, therefore, cannot do well without sympathy and flattery. It is accordingly very much against the grain that they remain long on the unpopular side of the question. They do not like to be shut out when laurels are to be given away at Court—or places under Government to be disposed of, in romantic situations in the country. They are happy to be reconciled on the first opportunity to prince and people, and to exchange their principles for a pension. They have not always strength of mind to think for themselves; nor courage enough to bear the unjust stigma of the opinions they have taken upon trust from others. Truth alone does not satisfy their pampered appetites, without the sauce of praise. To prefer truth to all other things, it requires that the mind should have been at some pains in finding it out, and that we should feel a severe delight in the contemplation of truth, seen by its own clear light, and not as it is reflected in the admiring eyes of the world. A philosopher may perhaps make a shift to be contented with the sober draughts of reason: a poet must have the applause of the world to intoxicate him. Milton was, however, a poet, and an honest man; he was Cromwell's secretary.

– The *Times* Newspaper: On the Connexion Between Toad-Eaters and Tyrants –

First published *Examiner*, 12 January 1817; reproduced from *Political Essays* (1819). This is principally an attack on Hazlitt's brother-in-law, John Stoddart. In his youth Stoddart was a disciple of the radical philosopher, William Godwin, but after Napoleon's defeat at Waterloo he supported reinstatement of the Bourbons to hereditary monarchies in France, Italy and Spain, and said so in numerous articles written for *The Times*. Weeks before Hazlitt wrote this essay, Stoddart had been sacked by John Walter the second, the paper's proprietor, for the ultra-royalist content of his leaders, but that did not discourage Hazlitt, in the penultimate paragraph of this essay, of reminding Stoddart what a true Jacobin was.

> 'Doubtless, the pleasure is as great
> In being cheated as to cheat.'

Jan. 12, 1817

We some time ago promised our friend, Mr Robert Owen, an explanation of some of the causes which impede the natural progress of liberty and human happiness. We have in part redeemed this pledge in what we said about *Coriolanus*, and we shall try in this article to redeem it still more. We grant to our ingenious and romantic friend, that the progress of knowledge and civilization is in itself favourable to liberty and equality, and that the general stream of thought and opinion constantly sets in this way, till power finds the tide of public feeling becoming too strong for it, ready to sap its rotten foundations, and 'bore through its castle-walls;' and then it contrives to turn the tide of knowledge and sentiment clean the contrary way, and either bribes human reason to take part against human nature, or knocks it on the head by a more summary process. Thus, in the year 1792, Mr Burke became a pensioner for writing his book against the French Revolution, and Mr Thomas Paine was outlawed for his *Rights of Man.* Since that period, the press has been the great enemy of freedom, the whole weight of that immense engine (for the purposes of good or ill) having a fatal bias given to it by the two main springs of fear and favour.

The weak sides of human intellect, by which power effects its conversion to the worst purposes, when it finds the exercise of free opinion inconsistent with the existence and uncontrolled exercise of arbitrary power, are these four, *viz.* the grossness of the imagination, which is seduced by outward appearances from the pursuit of real ultimate good; the subtlety of the understanding itself, which palliates by flimsy sophistry the most flagrant abuses; interest and advancement in the world; and lastly, the feuds and jealousies of literary men among one another. There is no class of persons so little calculated to act in *corps* as literary men. All their views are recluse and separate (for the mind acts by individual energy, and not by numbers): their motives, whether good or bad, are personal to themselves, their vanity exclusive, their love of truth independent; they exist not by the preservation, but the destruction of their own species; they are governed not by the spirit of unanimity, but of contradiction. They will hardly allow any thing to be right or any thing to be wrong, unless they are the first to find out that it is so; and are ready to prove the best things in the world the worst, and the worst the best, from the pure impulse of splenetic over-weening self-opinion, much more if they are likely to be well paid for it—not that interest is their ruling passion, but still it operates, silent and unseen, with them as with other men, when it can make a compromise with their vanity. This part of the character of men of letters is so well known, that Shakespear makes Brutus protest against the fitness of Cicero to be included in their enterprize on this very principle:—

> 'Oh, name him not: let us not break with him;
> For he will never follow any thing,
> That other men begin.'

The whole of Mr Burke's *Reflections on the French Revolution** is but an elaborate and damning comment on this short text. He quarrelled with the French Revolution out of spite to Rousseau, the spark of whose genius had kindled the flame of liberty in a nation. He therefore endeavoured to extinguish the flame—to put out the light; and he succeeded, because there were others like himself, ready to sacrifice every manly and generous principle to the morbid, sickly, effeminate, little, selfish, irritable, dirty spirit of authorship. Not only did such persons, according to Mr Coleridge's valuable and competent testimony (see his *Lay Sermon*) make the distinction between Atheism and Religion a mere stalking-horse for the indulgence of their idle vanity, but they made the other questions of Liberty and Slavery, of the Rights of Man, or the Divine Right of Kings to rule millions of men as their Slaves for ever, they made these vital and paramount questions (which whoever wilfully and knowingly compromises, is a traitor to himself and his species), subordinate to the low, whiffling, contemptible gratification of their literary jealousy. We shall not go over the painful list of instances; neither can we forget them. But they all or almost all contrived to sneak over one by one to the side on which 'empty praise or solid pudding' was to be got; they could not live without the smiles of the great

* When this work was first published, the King had copies of it bound in Morocco, and gave them away to his favourite courtiers, saying, 'It was a book which every gentleman ought to read.'

— *On the Connexion Between Toad-Eaters and Tyrants* —

(not they), nor provide for an increasing establishment without a loss of character; instead of going into some profitable business and exchanging their lyres for ledgers, their pens for the plough (the honest road to riches), they chose rather to prostitute their pens to the mock-heroic defence of the most bare-faced of all mummeries, the pretended alliance of kings and people! We told them how it would be, if they succeeded; it has turned out just as we said; and a pretty figure do these companions of Ulysses (*Compagnons du Lys*), these gaping converts to despotism, these well-fed victims of the charms of the Bourbons, now make, nestling under their laurels in the stye of Corruption, and sunk in torpid repose (from which they do not like to be disturbed by calling on their former names or professions), in lazy sinecures and good warm berths! Such is the history and mystery of literary patriotism and prostitution for the last twenty years.—Power is subject to none of these disadvantages. It is one and indivisible; it is self-centered, self-willed, incorrigible, inaccessible to temptation or entreaty; interest is on its side, passion is on its side, prejudice is on its side, the name of religion is on its side; the qualms of conscience it is not subject to, for it is iron-nerved; humanity it is proof against, for it sets itself up above humanity; reason it does not hearken to, except that reason which panders to its will and flatters its pride. It pursues its steady way, its undeviating everlasting course, 'unslacked of motion,' like that foul Indian idol, the Jaggernaut, and crushes poor upstart poets, patriots, and philosophers (the beings of an hour) and the successive never-ending generations of fools and knaves, beneath its feet; and mankind bow their willing necks to the yoke, and eagerly consign their children and their children's children to be torn in pieces by its scythe, or trampled to death by the gay, gaudy, painted, blood-stained wheels of the grim idol of power!

Such is the state of the eastern world, where the inherent baseness of man's nature, and his tendency to social order, to tyrannize and to be tyrannized over, has had full time to develop itself. Our turn seems next. We are but just setting out, it is true, in this bye-nook and corner of the world—but just recovering from the effects of the Revolution of 1688, and the defeated Rebellions of the years 1715 and 1745, but we need hardly despair under the auspices of the Editor of *The Times*, and with the example of the defeat 'of the last successful instance of a democratic rebellion,' by the second restoration of the Bourbons, before our eyes and close under our noses. Mr Owen may think the example of New Lanark more inviting, but the persons to whom he has dedicated his work turn their eyes another way!*

---

* Our loyal Editor used to bluster a great deal some time ago about putting down James Madison, and 'the last example of democratic rebellion in America.' In this he was consistent and logical. Could he not, however, find out another example of this same principle, by going a little farther back in history, and coming a little nearer home? If he has forgotten this chapter in our history, others who have profited

— *On the Connexion Between Toad-Eaters and Tyrants* —

Man is a toad-eating animal. The admiration of power in others is as common to man as the love of it in himself: the one makes him a tyrant, the other a slave. It is not he alone, who wears the golden crown, that is proud of it: the wretch who pines in a dungeon, and in chains, is dazzled with it; and if he could but shake off his own fetters, would care little about the wretches whom he left behind him, so that he might have an opportunity, on being set free himself, of gazing at this glittering gewgaw 'on some high holiday of once a year.' The slave, who has no other hope or consolation, clings to the apparition of royal magnificence, which insults his misery and his despair; stares through the hollow eyes of famine at the insolence of pride and luxury which has occasioned it, and hugs his chains the closer, because he has nothing else left. The French, under the old regime, made the glory of their *Grand Monarque* a set-off against rags and hunger, equally satisfied with *shows or bread*; and the poor Spaniard, delivered from temporary to permanent oppression, looks up once more with pious awe, to the time-hallowed towers of the Holy Inquisition. As the herd of mankind are stripped of every thing, in body and mind, so are they thankful for what is left; as is the desolation of their hearts and the wreck of their little all, so is the pomp and pride which is built upon their ruin, and their fawning admiration of it.

---

more by it have not. He may understand what we mean, by turning to the story of the two elder Blifils in *Tom Jones.*

'I've heard of hearts unkind, kind deeds
With coldness still returning:
Alas! the gratitude of men
Has oftener set me mourning.'*

There is something in the human mind, which requires an object for it to repose on; and, driven from all other sources of pride or pleasure, it falls in love with misery, and grows enamoured of oppression. It gazes after the liberty, the happiness, the comfort, the knowledge, which have been torn from it by the unfeeling gripe of wealth and power, as the poor debtor gazes with envy and wonder at the Lord Mayor's show. Thus is the world by degrees reduced to a spital or lazar-house, where the people waste away with want and disease, and are thankful if they are only suffered to crawl forgotten to their graves. Just in proportion to the systematic tyranny exercised over a nation, to its loss of a sense of freedom and the spirit of resistance, will be its loyalty; the most abject submission will always be rendered to the most confirmed despotism. The most wretched slaves are the veriest sycophants. The lacquey, mounted behind his master's coach, looks down with contempt upon the mob, forgetting his own origin and his actual situation, and comparing

---

* *Simon Lee, the old Huntsman,* a tale by Mr Wordsworth, of which he himself says,

'It is no tale, but if you think,
Perhaps a tale you'll make it.'

In this view it is a tale indeed, not 'of other times,' but of these.

— *On the Connexion Between Toad-Eaters and Tyrants* —

them only with that standard of gentility which he has perpetually in his eye. The hireling of the press (a still meaner slave) wears his livery, and is proud of it. He measures the greatness of others by his own meanness; their lofty pretensions indemnify him for his servility; he magnifies the sacredness of their persons to cover the laxity of his own principles. He offers up his own humanity, and that of all men, at the shrine of royalty. He sneaks to court; and the bland accents of power close his ears to the voice of freedom ever after; its velvet touch makes his heart marble to a people's sufferings. He is the intellectual pimp of power, as others are the practical ones of the pleasures of the great, and often on the same disinterested principle. For one tyrant, there are a thousand ready slaves. Man is naturally a worshipper of idols and a lover of kings. It is the excess of individual power, that strikes and gains over his imagination: the general misery and degradation which are the necessary consequences of it, are spread too wide, they lie too deep, their weight and import are too great, to appeal to any but the slow, inert, speculative, imperfect faculty of reason. The cause of liberty is lost in its own truth and magnitude; while the cause of despotism flourishes, triumphs, and is irresistible in the gross mixture, the *Belle Alliance*, of pride and ignorance.

Power is the grim idol that the world adores; that arms itself with destruction, and reigns by terror in the coward heart of man; that dazzles the senses, haunts the imagination, confounds the understanding, and tames the will, by the vastness of its pretensions, and the very hopelessness of resistance to them. Nay more, the more mischievous and extensive the tyranny—the longer it has lasted, and the longer it is likely to last—the stronger is the hold it takes of the minds of its victims, the devotion to it increasing with the dread. It does not satisfy the enormity of the appetite for servility, till it has slain the mind of a nation, and becomes like the evil principle of the universe, from which there is no escape. So in some countries, the most destructive animals are held sacred, despair and terror completely overpowering reason. The prejudices of superstition (religion is another name for fear) are always the strongest in favour of those forms of worship which require the most bloody sacrifices; the foulest idols are those which are approached with the greatest awe; for it should seem that those objects are the most sacred to passion and imagination, which are the most revolting to reason and common sense. No wonder that the Editor of *The Times* bows his head before the idol of Divine Right, or of Legitimacy, (as he calls it) which has had more lives sacrificed to its ridiculous and unintelligible pretensions, in the last twenty-five years, than were ever sacrificed to any other idol in all preceding ages. Never was there any thing so well contrived as this fiction of Legitimacy, to suit the fastidious delicacy of modern sycophants. It hits their grovelling servility and petulant egotism exactly between wind and water.

— On the Connexion Between Toad-Eaters and Tyrants —

The contrivers or re-modellers of this idol, beat all other idol-mongers, whether Jews, Gentiles or Christians, hollow. The principle of all idolatry is the same: it is the want of something to admire, without knowing what or why: it is the love of an effect without a cause; it is a voluntary tribute of admiration which does not compromise our vanity: it is setting something up over all the rest of the world, to which we feel ourselves to be superior, for it is our own handiwork; so that the more perverse the homage we pay to it, the more it pampers our self-will: the meaner the object, the more magnificent and pompous the attributes we bestow upon it; the greater the lie, the more enthusiastically it is believed and greedily swallowed:—

> 'Of whatsoever race his godhead be,
> Stock, stone, or other homely pedigree,
> In his defence his servants are as bold
> As if he had been made of beaten gold.'

In this inverted ratio, the bungling impostors of former times, and less refined countries, got no further than stocks and stones: their utmost stretch of refinement in absurdity went no further than to select the most mischievous animals or the most worthless objects for the adoration of their besotted votaries: but the framers of the new law-fiction of legitimacy have started a nonentity. The ancients sometimes worshipped the sun or stars, or deified heroes and great

— ALL THAT IS WORTH REMEMBERING —

men: the moderns have found out the image of the divinity in Louis XVIII! They have set up an object for their idolatry, which they themselves must laugh at, if hypocrisy were not with them the most serious thing in the world. They offer up thirty millions of men to it as its victims, and yet they know that it is nothing but a scarecrow to keep the world in subjection to their renegado whimsies and preposterous hatred of the liberty and happiness of mankind. They do not think kings gods, but they make believe that they do so, to degrade their fellows to the rank of brutes. Legitimacy answers every object of their meanness and malice—*omne tulit punctum.*—This mock-doctrine, this little Hunchback, which our resurrection-men, the Humane Society of Divine Right, have foisted on the altar of Liberty, is not only a phantom of the imagination, but a contradiction in terms; it is a prejudice, but an exploded prejudice; it is an imposture, that imposes on nobody; it is powerful only in impotence, safe in absurdity, courted from fear and hatred, a dead prejudice linked to the living mind; the sink of honour, the grave of liberty, a palsy in the heart of a nation; it claims the species as its property, and derives its right neither from God nor man; not from the authority of the Church, which it treats cavalierly, and yet in contempt of the will of the people, which it scouts as opposed to its own: its two chief supporters are the sword of the Duke of Wellington and the pen of the Editor of *The Times*! The last of these props has, we understand, just failed it.

— *On the Connexion Between Toad-Eaters and Tyrants* —

We formerly gave the Editor of *The Times* a definition of a true Jacobin, as one 'who had seen the evening star set over a poor man's cottage, and connected it with the hope of human happiness.' The city-politician laughed this pastoral definition to scorn, and nicknamed the person who had very innocently laid it down, 'the true Jacobin who writes in the *Chronicle*,'— a nickname by which we profited as little as he has by our Illustrations. Since that time our imagination has grown a little less romantic: so we will give him another, which he may chew the cud upon at his leisure. A true Jacobin, then, is one who does not believe in the divine right of kings, or in any other *alias* for it, which implies that they reign 'in contempt of the will of the people;' and he holds all such kings to be tyrants, and their subjects slaves. To be a true Jacobin, a man must be a good hater; but this is the most difficult and the least amiable of all the virtues: the most trying and the most thankless of all tasks. The love of liberty consists in the hatred of tyrants. The true Jacobin hates the enemies of liberty as they hate liberty, with all his strength and with all his might, and with all his heart and with all his soul. His memory is as long, and his will as strong as theirs, though his hands are shorter. He never forgets or forgives an injury done to the people, for tyrants never forget or forgive one done to themselves. There is no love lost between them. He does not leave them the sole benefit of their old motto, *Odia in longum jaciens quae conderet auctaque promeret.* He

39

makes neither peace nor truce with them. His hatred of wrong only ceases with the wrong. The sense of it, and of the barefaced assumption of the right to inflict it, deprives him of his rest. It stagnates in his blood. It loads his heart with aspics' tongues, deadly to venal pens. It settles in his brain—it puts him beside himself. Who will not feel all this for girl, a toy, a turn of the dice, a word, a blow, for any thing relating to himself; and will not the friend of liberty feel as much for mankind? The love of truth is a passion in his mind, as the love of power is a passion in the minds of others. Abstract reason, unassisted by passion, is no match for power and prejudice, armed with force and cunning. The love of liberty is the love of others; the love of power is the love of ourselves. The one is real; the other often but an empty dream. Hence the defection of modern apostates. While they are looking about, wavering and distracted, in pursuit of universal good or universal fame, the eye of power is upon them, like the eye of Providence, that neither slumbers nor sleeps, and that watches but for one object, its own good. They take no notice of it at first, but it is still upon them, and never off them. It at length catches theirs, and they bow to its sacred light; and like the poor fluttering bird, quail beneath it, are seized with a vertigo, and drop senseless into its jaws, that close upon them for ever, and so we see no more of them, which is well.

'And we saw three poets in a dream, walking up and down on the face of the earth, and holding in their hands a human heart, which, as they raised their eyes to heaven, they kissed and worshipped; and a mighty shout arose and shook the air, for the towers of the Bastile had fallen, and a nation had become, of slaves, freemen; and the three poets, as they heard the sound, leaped and shouted, and made merry, and their voice was choked with tears of joy, which they shed over the human heart, which they kissed and worshipped. And not long after, we saw the same three poets, the one with a receipt-stamp in his hand, the other with a laurel on his head, and the third with a symbol which we could make nothing of, for it was neither literal nor allegorical, following in the train of the Pope and the Inquisition and the Bourbons, and worshipping the mark of the Beast, with the emblem of the human heart thrown beneath their feet, which they trampled and spit upon!'—This apologue is not worth finishing, nor are the people to whom it relates worth talking of. We have done with them.

– On Egotism –

Probably composed soon after Napoleon's death (that is, within a month or so of 5 May 1821) and first published in the Paris edition of *Table Talk*, which appeared in 1825; reproduced here from *The Plain Speaker* (1826). Egotism is for modern readers a largely negative trait but to Hazlitt it was the concomitant of genius – a quality he attributed to Wordsworth, Milton and Rembrandt, among others. His task in this essay is to distinguish what is good about egotism from such vices as pride, vanity, and contempt.

It is mentioned in the *Life of Salvator Rosa*, that on the occasion of an altar-piece of his being exhibited at Rome, in the triumph of the moment, he compared himself to Michael Angelo, and spoke against Raphael, calling him *hard*, *dry*, &c. Both these were fatal symptoms for the ultimate success of the work: the picture was in fact afterwards severely censured, so as to cause him much uneasiness; and he passed a great part of his life in quarrelling with the world for admiring his landscapes, which were truly excellent, and for not admiring his historical pieces, which were full of defects. Salvator wanted self-knowledge, and that respect for others, which is both a cause and consequence of it.

— *On Egotism* —

Like many more, he mistook the violent and irritable workings of self-will (in a wrong direction) for the impulse of genius, and his insensibility to the vast superiority of others for a proof of his equality with them.

In the first place, nothing augurs worse for any one's pretensions to the highest rank of excellence than his making free with those of others. He who boldly and unreservedly places himself on a level with the *mighty dead,* shows a want of sentiment—the only thing that can ensure immortality to his own works. When we forestall the judgment of posterity, it is because we are not confident of it. A mind that brings all others into a line with its own naked or assumed merits, that sees all objects in the foreground as it were, that does not regard the lofty monuments of genius through the atmosphere of fame, is coarse, crude, and repulsive as a picture without aerial perspective. Time, like distance, spreads a haze and a glory round all things. Not to perceive this, is to want a sense, is to be without imagination. Yet there are those who strut in their own self-opinion, and deck themselves out in the plumes of fancied self-importance as if they were crowned with laurel by Apollo's own hand. There was nothing in common between Salvator and Michael Angelo: if there had, the consciousness of the power with which he had to contend would have over-awed and struck him dumb; so that the very familiarity of his approaches proved (as much as any thing else) the immense distance placed between them. Painters alone seem to have a trick of putting themselves on an equal footing with the greatest of their predecessors, of advancing, on the sole strength of their vanity and presumption, to the highest seats in the Temple of Fame, of talking of themselves and Raphael and Michael Angelo in the same breath! What should we think of a poet who should publish to the world, or give a broad hint in private, that he conceived himself fully on a par with Homer or Milton or Shakespear? It would be too much for a friend to say so of him. But artists suffer their friends to puff them in the true 'King Cambyses' vein' without blushing. Is it that they are often men without a liberal education, who have no notion of any thing that does not come under their immediate observation, and who accordingly prefer the living to the dead, and themselves to all the rest of the world? Or that there is something in the nature of the profession itself, fixing the view on a particular point of time, and not linking the present either with the past or future?

Again, Salvator's disregard for Raphael, instead of inspiring him with any thing like 'vain and self-conceit,' ought to have taught him the greatest diffidence in himself. Instead of anticipating a triumph over Raphael from this circumstance, he might have foreseen in it the sure source of his mortification and defeat. The public looked to find in *his* pictures what he did not see in Raphael, and were necessarily disappointed. He could hardly be expected to produce that which when produced and set before him, he did not feel or

— *On Egotism* —

understand. The genius for a particular thing does not imply taste in general or for other things, but it assuredly presupposes a taste or feeling for that particular thing. Salvator was so much offended with the *dryness*, *hardness*, &c. of Raphael, only because he was not struck, that is, did not sympathise with the divine mind within. If he had, he would have bowed as at a shrine, in spite of the homeliness or finicalness of the covering. Let no man build himself a spurious self-esteem on his contempt or indifference for acknowledged excellence. He will in the end pay dear for a momentary delusion: for the world will sooner or later discover those deficiencies in him, which render him insensible to all merits but his own.

Of all modes of acquiring distinction and, as it were, 'getting the start of the majestic world,' the most absurd as well as disgusting is that of setting aside the claims of others in the lump, and holding out our own particular excellence or pursuit as the only one worth attending to. We thus set ourselves up as the standard of perfection, and treat every thing else that diverges from that standard as beneath our notice. At this rate, a contempt for any thing and a superiority to it are synonymous. It is a cheap and a short way of showing that we possess all excellence within ourselves, to deny the use or merit of all those qualifications that do not belong to us. According to such a mode of computation, it would appear that our value is to be estimated not by the number of acquirements that we *do* possess, but of those in which we are deficient and to which we are insensible:—so that we can at any time supply the place of wisdom and skill by a due proportion of ignorance, affectation, and conceit. If so, the dullest fellow, with impudence enough to despise what he does not understand, will always be the brightest genius and the greatest man. If stupidity is to be a substitute for taste, knowledge, and genius, any one may dogmatise and play the critic on this ground. We may easily make a monopoly of talent, if the torpedo-touch of our callous and wilful indifference is to neutralise all other pretensions. We have only to deny the advantages of others to make them our own: illiberality will carve out the way to pre-eminence much better than toil or study or quickness of parts; and by narrowing our views and divesting ourselves at last of common feeling and humanity, we may arrogate every valuable accomplishment to ourselves, and exalt ourselves vastly above our fellow-mortals! That is, in other words, we have only to shut our eyes, in order to blot the sun out of heaven, and to annihilate whatever gives light or heat to the world, if it does not emanate from one single source, by spreading the cloud of our own envy, spleen, malice, want of comprehension, and prejudice over it. Yet how many are there who act upon this theory in good earnest, grow more bigoted to it every day, and not only become the dupes of it themselves, but by dint of gravity, by bullying and brow-beating, succeed in making converts of others!

— *On Egotism* —

A man is a political economist. Good: but this is no reason he should think there is nothing else in the world, or that every thing else is good for nothing. Let us suppose that this is the most important subject, and that being his favourite study, he is the best judge of that point, still it is not the only one—why then treat every other question or pursuit with disdain as insignificant and mean, or endeavour to put others who have devoted their whole time to it out of conceit with that on which they depend for their amusement or (perhaps) subsistence? I see neither the wit, wisdom, nor good-nature of this mode of proceeding. Let him fill his library with books on this one subject, yet other persons are not bound to follow the example, and exclude every other topic from theirs—let him write, let him talk, let him think on nothing else, but let him not impose the same pedantic humour as a duty or a mark of taste on others—let him ride the high horse, and drag his heavy load of mechanical knowledge along the iron railway of the master-science, but let him not move out of it to taunt or jostle those who are jogging quietly along upon their several *hobbies,* who 'owe him no allegiance,' and care not one jot for his opinion. Yet we could forgive such a person, if he made it his boast that he had read *Don Quixote* twice through in the original Spanish, and preferred *Lycidas* to all Milton's smaller poems! What would Mr Mill say to any one who should profess a contempt for political economy? He would answer very bluntly and very properly,

'Then you know nothing about it.' It is a pity that so sensible a man and close a reasoner should think of putting down other lighter and more elegant pursuits by professing a contempt or indifference for them, which springs from precisely the same source, and is of just the same value. But so it is that there seems to be a tacit presumption of folly in whatever gives pleasure; while an air of gravity and wisdom hovers round the painful and pedantic!

A man comes into a room, and on his first entering, declares without preface or ceremony his contempt for poetry. Are we therefore to conclude him a greater genius than Homer? No: but by this cavalier opinion he assumes a certain natural ascendancy over those who admire poetry. To *look down* upon any thing seemingly implies a greater elevation and enlargement of view than to *look up* to it. The present Lord Chancellor took upon him to declare in open court that he would not go across the street to hear Madame Catalani sing. What did this prove? His want of an ear for music, not his capacity for any thing higher. So far as it went, it only showed him to be inferior to those thousands of persons who go with eager expectation to hear her, and come away with astonishment and rapture. A man might as well tell you he is deaf, and expect you to look at him with more respect. The want of any external sense or organ is an acknowledged defect and infirmity: the want of an internal sense or faculty is equally so, though our self-love contrives to give a

— *On Egotism* —

different turn to it. We mortify others by *throwing cold water* on that in which they have an advantage over us, or stagger their opinion of an excellence which is not of self-evident or absolute utility, and lessen its supposed value, by limiting the universality of a taste for it. Lord Eldon's protest on this occasion was the more extraordinary, as he is not only a good-natured but a successful man. These little spiteful allusions are most apt to proceed from disappointed vanity, and an apprehension that justice is not done to ourselves. By being at the top of a profession, we have leisure to look beyond it. Those who really excel and are allowed to excel in any thing have no excuse for trying to gain a reputation by undermining the pretensions of others; they stand on their own ground; and do not need the aid of invidious comparisons. Besides, the consciousness of excellence produces a fondness for, a faith in it. I should half suspect that any one could not be a great lawyer, who denied that Madame Catalani was a great singer. The Chancellor must dislike her decisive tone, the rapidity of her movements! The late Chancellor (Erskine) was a man of (at least) a different stamp. In the exuberance and buoyancy of his animal spirits, he scattered the graces and ornaments of life over the dust and cobwebs of the law. What is there that is now left of him—what is there to redeem his foibles, or to recall the flush of early enthusiasm in his favour, or kindle one spark of sympathy in the breast, but his romantic admiration of Mrs Siddons? There are those who, if you praise Walton's *Complete Angler*, sneer at it as a childish or old-womanish performance: some laugh at the amusement of fishing as silly, others carp at it as cruel; and Dr Johnson said that 'a fishing-rod was a stick with a hook at one end, and a fool at the other.' I would rather take the word of one who had stood for days, up to his knees in water, and in the coldest weather, intent on this employ, who returned to it again with unabated relish, and who spent his whole life in the same manner without being weary of it at last. There is something in this more than Dr Johnson's definition accounts for. A *fool* takes no interest in any thing; or if he does, it is better to be a fool, than a wise man, whose only pleasure is to disparage the pursuits and occupations of others, and out of ignorance or prejudice to condemn them, merely because they are not *his*.

Whatever interests, is interesting. I know of no way of estimating the real value of objects in all their bearings and consequences, but I can tell at once their intellectual value by the degree of passion or sentiment the very idea and mention of them excites in the mind. To judge of things by reason or the calculations of positive utility is a slow, cold, uncertain, and barren process—their power of appealing to and affecting the imagination as subjects of thought and feeling is best measured by the habitual impression they leave upon the mind, and it is with this only we have to do in expressing our delight or admiration of them, or in setting a just mental value upon them. They ought to

— *On Egotism* —

excite all the emotion which they do excite; for this is the instinctive and unerring result of the constant experience we have had of their power of affecting us, and of the associations that cling unconsciously to them. Fancy, feeling may be very inadequate tests of truth; but truth itself operates chiefly on the human mind through them. It is in vain to tell me that what excites the heart-felt sigh of youth, the tears of delight in age, and fills up the busy interval between with pleasing and lofty thoughts, is frivolous, or a waste of time, or of no use. You only by that give me a mean opinion of your ideas of utility. The labour of years, the triumph of aspiring genius and consummate skill, is not to be put down by a cynical frown, by a supercilious smile, by an ignorant sarcasm. Things barely of use are subjects of professional skill and scientific inquiry: they must also be beautiful and pleasing to attract common attention, and be naturally and universally interesting. A pair of shoes is good to wear: a pair of sandals is a more picturesque object; and a statue or a poem are certainly good to think and talk about, which are part of the business of life. To think and speak of them with contempt is therefore a wilful and studied solecism. Pictures are good things to go and see. This is what people do; they do not expect to eat or make a dinner of them; but we sometimes want to fill up the time before dinner. The progress of civilisation and refinement is from instrumental to final causes; from supplying the wants of the body to providing luxuries for the mind.

To stop at the *mechanical,* and refuse to proceed to the *fine arts,* or churlishly to reject all ornamental studies and elegant accomplishments as mean and trivial, because they only afford employment to the imagination, create food for thought, furnish the mind, sustain the soul in health and enjoyment, is a rude and barbarous theory—

'Et propter vitam vivendi perdere causas.'

Before we absolutely condemn any thing, we ought to be able to show something better, not merely in itself, but in the same class. To know the best in each class infers a higher degree of taste; to reject the class is only a negation of taste; for different classes do not interfere with one another, nor can any one's *ipse dixit* be taken on so wide a question as abstract excellence. Nothing is truly and altogether despicable that excites angry contempt or warm opposition, since this always implies that someone else is of a different opinion, and takes an equal interest in it.

When I speak of what is interesting, however, I mean not only to a particular profession, but in general to others. Indeed, it is the very popularity and obvious interest attached to certain studies and pursuits, that excites the envy and hostile regard of graver and more recondite professions. Man is perhaps not naturally an egotist, or at least he is satisfied with his own particular line of excellence and the value that he supposes inseparable from it, till he comes into the world and finds it of so little account in the eyes of the vulgar; and he then turns round and vents his chagrin and disappointment on those more attractive, but (as he conceives) superficial studies, which cost less labour and patience to understand them, and are of so much less use to society. The injustice done to ourselves makes us unjust to others. The man of science and the hard student (from this cause, as well as from a certain unbending hardness of mind) come at last to regard whatever is generally pleasing and striking as worthless and light, and to proportion their contempt to the admiration of others; while the artist, the poet, and the votary of pleasure and popularity treat the more solid and useful branches of human knowledge as disagreeable and dull. This is often carried to too great a length. It is enough that 'wisdom is justified of her children:' the philosopher ought to smile, instead of being angry at the folly of mankind (if such it is), and those who find both pleasure and profit in adorning and polishing the airy 'capitals' of science and of art, ought not to grudge those who toil underground at the foundation, the praise that is due to their patience and self-denial. There is a variety of tastes and capacities that requires all the variety of men's talents to administer to it. The less excellent must be provided for as well as the more excellent. Those who are only capable of amusement ought to be amused. If all men were forced to be great philosophers and lasting benefactors of their species, how few of us could ever do any thing at all! But nature acts more impartially, though not improvidently. Wherever she bestows a *turn* for any thing on the individual, she implants a corresponding taste for it in others. We have only to 'throw our bread upon the waters, and after many days we shall find it again.' Let us do our best, and we need not be ashamed of the smallness of our talent, or afraid of the calumnies and contempt of envious maligners. When Goldsmith was talking one day to Sir Joshua of writing a fable in which little fishes were to be introduced, Dr Johnson rolled about uneasily in his seat and began to laugh, on which Goldsmith said rather angrily—'Why do you laugh? If you were to write a fable for little fishes, you would make them speak like great whales!' The reproof was just. Johnson was in truth conscious of Goldsmith's superior inventiveness, and of the lighter graces of his pen, but he wished to reduce every thing to his own pompous and oracular style. There are not only *books for children*, but books for all ages and for both sexes. After we grow up to years of discretion, we do not all become equally wise at once. Our own tastes change: the tastes of other individuals are still more different. It was said the other day, that 'Thomson's Seasons would be read while there was a boarding-school girl in the world.' If a thousand volumes were written against Hervey's *Meditations,* the *Meditations* would be read when the criticisms were forgotten. To the illiterate and vain, affectation and verbiage will always pass for

— *On Egotism* —

fine writing, while the world stands. No woman ever liked Burke, or disliked Goldsmith. It is idle to set up an universal standard. There is a large class who, in spite of themselves, prefer Westall or Angelica Kaufmann to Raphael; nor is it fit they should do otherwise. We may come to something like a fixed and exclusive standard of taste, if we confine ourselves to what will please the best judges, meaning thereby persons of the most refined and cultivated minds, and by persons of the most refined and cultivated minds, generally meaning *ourselves*!*

To return to the original question. I can conceive of nothing so little or ridiculous as pride. It is a mixture of insensibility and ill-nature, in which it is hard to say which has the largest share. If a man knows or excels in, or has ever studied any two things, I will venture to affirm he will be proud of neither. It is perhaps excusable for a person who is ignorant of all but one thing, to think *that* the sole excellence, and to be full of himself as the possessor. The way to cure him of this folly is to give him something else to be proud of. Vanity is a building that falls to the ground as you widen its foundation, or strengthen the props that should support it. The greater a man is, the less he necessarily thinks of himself, for his knowledge enlarges with his

---

* The books that we like in youth we return to in age, if there is nature and simplicity in them. At what age should *Robinson Crusoe* be laid aside? I do not think that *Don Quixote* is a book for children; or at least, they understand it better as they grow up.

attainments. In himself he feels that he is nothing, a point, a speck in the universe, except as his mind reflects that universe, and as he enters into the infinite variety of truth, beauty, and power contained in it. Let any one be brought up among books, and taught to think words the only things, and he may conceive highly of himself from the proficiency he has made in language and in letters. Let him then be compelled to attempt some other pursuit—painting, for instance—and be made to feel the difficulties, the refinements of which it is capable, and the number of things of which he was utterly ignorant before, and there will be an end of his pedantry and his pride together. Nothing but the want of comprehension of view or generosity of spirit can make any one fix on his own particular acquirement as the limit of all excellence. No one is (generally speaking) great in more than one thing—if he extends his pursuits, he dissipates his strength—yet in that one thing how small is the interval between him and the next in merit and reputation to himself! But he thinks nothing of, or scorns or loathes the name of his rival, so that all that the other possesses in common goes for nothing, and the fraction of a difference between them constitutes (in his opinion) the sum and substance of all that is excellent in the universe! Let a man be wise, and then let us ask, will his wisdom make him proud? Let him excel all others in the graces of the mind, has he also those of the body? He has the advantage of fortune, but has he also that of birth, or if he has both,

— *On Egotism* —

has he health, strength, beauty in a supreme degree? Or have not others the same, or does he think all these nothing because he does not possess them? The proud man fancies that there is no one worth regarding but himself: he might as well fancy there is no other being but himself. The one is not a greater stretch of madness than the other. To make pride justifiable, there ought to be but one proud man in the world, for if any one individual has a right to be so, nobody else has. So far from thinking ourselves superior to all the rest of the species, we cannot be sure that we are above the meanest and most despised individual of it: for he may have some virtue, some excellence, some source of happiness or usefulness within himself, which may redeem all other disadvantages: or even if he is without any such hidden worth, this is not a subject of exultation, but of regret, to any one tinctured with the smallest humanity, and he who is totally devoid of the latter, cannot have much reason to be proud of any thing else. Arkwright, who invented the spinning-jenny, for many years kept a paltry barber's shop in a provincial town: yet at that time that wonderful machinery was working in his brain, which has added more to the wealth and resources of this country than all the pride of ancestry or insolence of upstart nobility for the last hundred years. We should be cautious whom we despise. If we do not know them, we can have no right to pronounce a hasty sentence: if we do, they may espy some few defects in us. *No man is a hero to his valet-de-chambre.*

What is it then that makes the difference? The dress and pride. But he is the most of a hero who is least distinguished by the one, and most free from the other. If we enter into conversation upon equal terms with the lowest of the people, unrestrained by circumstance, unawed by interest, we shall find in ourselves but little superiority over them. If we know what they do not, they know what we do not. In general, those who do things for others, know more about them than those for whom they are done. A groom knows more about horses than his master. He rides them too: but the one rides behind, the other before! Hence the number of forms and ceremonies that have been invented to keep the magic circle of fancied self-importance inviolate. The late King sought but one interview with Dr Johnson: his present Majesty is never tired of the company of Mr Croker.

The collision of truth or genius naturally gives a shock to the pride of exalted rank: the great and mighty usually seek out the dregs of mankind, buffoons and flatterers, for their pampered self-love to repose on. Pride soon tires of every thing but its shadow, servility: but how poor a triumph is that which exists only by excluding all rivalry, however remote. He who invites competition (the only test of merit), who challenges fair comparisons, and weighs different claims, is alone possessed of manly ambition; but will not long continue vain or proud. Pride is 'a cell of ignorance; travelling a-bed.' If we look at all out of ourselves, we

— *On Egotism* —

must see how far short we are of what we would be thought. The man of genius is poor;* the rich man is not a lord: the lord wants to be a king: the king is uneasy to be a tyrant or a god. Yet he alone, who could claim this last character upon earth, gave his life a ransom for others! The dwarf in the romance, who saw the shadows of the fairest and the mightiest among the sons of men pass before him, that he might assume the shape he liked best, had only his choice of wealth, or beauty, or valour, or power. But could he have clutched them all, and melted them into one essence of pride, the triumph would not have been lasting. Could vanity take all pomp and power to itself, could it, like the rainbow, span the earth, and seem to prop the heavens, after all it would be but the wonder of the ignorant, the pageant of a moment. The fool who dreams that he is great should first forget that he is a man, and before he

---

* I do not speak of poverty as an absolute evil; though when accompanied with luxurious habits and vanity, it is a great one. Even hardships and privations have their use, and give strength and endurance. Labour renders ease delightful—hunger is the best sauce. The peasant, who at noon rests from his weary task under a hawthorn hedge, and eats his slice of coarse bread and cheese or rusty bacon, enjoys more real luxury than the prince with pampered, listless appetite under a canopy of state. Why then does the mind of man pity the former, and envy the latter? It is because the imagination changes places with others in situation only, not in feeling; and in fancying ourselves the peasant, we revolt at his homely fare, from not being possessed of his gross taste or keen appetite, while in thinking of the prince, we suppose ourselves to sit down to his delicate viands and sumptuous board, with a relish unabated by long habit and vicious excess. I am not sure whether Mandeville has not given the same answer to this hackneyed question.

thinks of being proud, should pray to be mad!—The only great man in modern times, that is, the only man who rose in deeds and fame to the level of antiquity, who might turn his gaze upon himself, and wonder at his height, for on him all eyes were fixed as his majestic stature towered above thrones and monuments of renown, died the other day in exile, and in lingering agony; and we still see fellows strutting about the streets, and fancying they are something!

Personal vanity is incompatible with the great and the *ideal*. He who has not seen, or thought, or read of something finer than himself, has seen, or read, or thought little; and he who has, will not be always looking in the glass of his own vanity. Hence poets, artists, and men of genius in general, are seldom coxcombs, but often slovens; for they find something out of themselves better worth studying than their own persons. They have an imaginary standard in their minds, with which ordinary features (even their own) will not bear a comparison, and they turn their thoughts another way. If a man had a face like one of Raphael's or Titian's heads, he might be proud of it, but not else; and, even then, he would be stared at as a *nondescript* by 'the universal English nation.' Few persons who have seen the Antinous or the Theseus will be much charmed with their own beauty or symmetry; nor will those who understand the *costume* of the antique, or Vandyke's dresses, spend much time in decking themselves out in all the deformity of the prevailing fashion. A coxcomb

— *On Egotism* —

is his own lay-figure, for want of any better models to employ his time and imagination upon.

There is an inverted sort of pride, the reverse of that egotism that has been above described, and which, because it cannot be every thing, is dissatisfied with every thing. A person who is liable to this infirmity, 'thinks nothing done, while any thing remains to be done.' The sanguine egotist prides himself on what he can do or possesses, the morbid egotist despises himself for what he wants, and is ever going out of his way to attempt hopeless and impossible tasks. The effect in either case is not at all owing to reason, but to temperament. The one is as easily depressed by what mortifies his latent ambition, as the other is elated by what flatters his immediate vanity. There are persons whom no success, no advantages, no applause can satisfy, for they dwell only on failure and defeat. They constantly 'forget the things that are behind, and press forward to the things that are before.' The greatest and most decided acquisitions would not indemnify them for the smallest deficiency. They go beyond the old motto—*Aut Caesar, aut nihil*—they not only want to be at the head of whatever they undertake, but if they succeed in that, they immediately want to be at the head of something else, no matter how gross or trivial. The charm that rivets their affections is not the importance or reputation annexed to the new pursuit, but its novelty or difficulty. That must be a wonderful accomplishment indeed, which baffles their skill—nothing is with them of any value but as it gives scope to their restless activity of mind, their craving after an uneasy and importunate state of excitement. To them the pursuit is every thing, the possession nothing. I have known persons of this stamp, who, with every reason to be satisfied with their success in life, and with the opinion entertained of them by others, despised themselves because they could not do something which they were not bound to do, and which, if they could have done it, would not have added one jot to their respectability, either in their own eyes or those of any one else, the very insignificance of the attainment irritating their impatience, for it is the humour of such dispositions to argue, 'If they cannot succeed in what is trifling and contemptible, how should they succeed in any thing else?' If they could make the circuit of the arts and sciences, and master them all, they would take to some mechanical exercise, and if they failed, be as discontented as ever. All that they can do vanishes out of sight the moment it is within their grasp, and 'nothing is but what is not.' A poet of this description is ambitious of the thews and muscles of a prize fighter, and thinks himself nothing without them. A prose writer would be a fine tennis-player, and is thrown into despair because he is not one, without considering that it requires a whole life devoted to the game to excel in it; and that, even if he could dispense with this apprenticeship, he would still be just as much bound to excel in rope-dancing, or

— *On Egotism* —

horsemanship, or playing at cup and ball like the Indian jugglers, all which is impossible. This feeling is a strange mixture of modesty and pride. We think nothing of what we are, because we cannot be every thing with a wish. Goldsmith was even jealous of beauty in the other sex, and the same character is attributed to Wharton by Pope:

> 'Though listening senates hung on all he spoke,
> The club must hail him master of the joke.'

Players are for going into the church—officers in the army turn players. For myself, do what I might, I should think myself a poor creature unless I could beat a boy of ten years old at chuck-farthing, or an elderly gentlewoman at piquet!

The extreme of fastidious discontent and repining is as bad as that of over-weening presumption. We ought to be satisfied if we have succeeded in any one thing, or with having done our best. Any thing more is for health and amusement, and should be resorted to as a source of pleasure, not of fretful impatience, and endless pity, self-imposed mortification. Perhaps the jealous, uneasy temperament is most favourable to continued exertion and improvement, if it does not lead us to fritter away attention on too many pursuits. By looking out of ourselves, we gain knowledge: by being little satisfied with what we have done, we are less apt to sink into indolence and security. To conclude

— ALL THAT IS WORTH REMEMBERING —

with a piece of egotism: I never begin one of these essays with a consciousness of having written a line before; and having got to the end of the volume, hope never to look into it again.

– On Reason and Imagination –

Written between 5 and 7 March 1822, first published *The Plain Speaker* (1826), from which the text given here is reproduced. In manuscript this essay was entitled 'On Individuality', and that is its subject: the importance of selfhood as gateway to moral truth.

I hate people who have no notion of anything but generalities, and forms, and creeds, and naked propositions, even worse than I dislike those who cannot for the soul of them arrive at the comprehension of an abstract idea. There are those (even among philosophers) who, deeming that all truth is contained within certain outlines and common topics, if you proceed to add colour or relief from individuality, protest against the use of rhetoric as an illogical thing; and if you drop a hint of pleasure or pain as ever entering into 'this breathing world,' raise a prodigious outcry against all appeals to the passions.

It is, I confess, strange to me that men who pretend to more than usual accuracy in distinguishing and analysing, should insist that in treating of human nature, of moral good and evil, the nominal differences are alone of any value, or that in describing the feelings and motives of men, any thing that conveys the smallest idea of what those feelings are in any given circumstances, or can by parity of reason ever be in any others, is a deliberate attempt at artifice and delusion—as if a knowledge or representation of things as they really exist (rules and definitions apart) was a proportionable departure from the truth. They stick to the table of contents, and never open the volume of the mind. They are for having maps, not pictures of the world we live in: as much as to say that a bird's-eye view of things contains the truth, the whole truth, and nothing but the truth. If you want to look for the situation of a particular spot, they turn to a pasteboard globe, on which they fix their wandering gaze; and because you cannot find the object of your search in their bald 'abridgements,' tell you there is no such place, or that it is not worth inquiring after. They had better confine their studies to the celestial sphere and the signs of the zodiac; for there they will meet with no petty details to boggle at, or contradict their vague conclusions. Such persons would make excellent theologians, but are very indifferent philosophers.—To pursue this geographical reasoning a little farther. They may say that the map of a county or shire, for instance, is too large, and conveys a disproportionate idea of its relation to the whole. And we say that their map of the globe is too small, and conveys no idea of it at all.

— *On Reason and Imagination* —

> 'In the world's volume
> Our Britain shows as of it, but not in it;
> In a great pool a swan's nest:'

but is it really so? What! the county is bigger than the map at any rate: the representation falls short of the reality, by a million degrees, and you would omit it altogether in order to arrive at a balance of power in the non-entities of the understanding, and call this keeping within the bounds of sense and reason; and whatever does not come within those self-made limits is to be set aside as frivolous or monstrous. But 'there are more things between heaven and earth than were ever dreamt of in this philosophy.' They cannot get them all in, *of the size of life*, and therefore they reduce them on a graduated scale, till they think they can. So be it, for certain necessary and general purposes, and in compliance with the infirmity of human intellect: but at other times, let us enlarge our conceptions to the dimensions of the original objects; nor let it be pretended that we have outraged truth and nature, because we have encroached on your diminutive mechanical standard. There is no language, no description that can strictly come up to the truth and force of reality: all we have to do is to guide our descriptions and conclusions by the reality. A certain proportion must be kept: we must not invert the rules of moral perspective. Logic should enrich and invigorate its decisions by the use of imagination; as rhetoric should be governed in its application,

— ALL THAT IS WORTH REMEMBERING —

and guarded from abuse by the checks of the understanding. Neither, I apprehend, is sufficient alone. The mind can conceive only one or a few things in their integrity: if it proceeds to more, it must have recourse to artificial substitutes, and judge by comparison merely. In the former case, it may select the least worthy, and so distort the truth of things, by giving a hasty preference: in the latter, the danger is that it may refine and abstract so much as to attach no idea at all to them, corresponding with their practical value, or their influence on the minds of those concerned with them. Men act from individual impressions; and to know mankind, we should be acquainted with nature. Men act from passion; and we can only judge of passion by sympathy. Persons of the dry and husky class above spoken of, often seem to think even nature itself an interloper on their flimsy theories. They prefer the shadows in Plato's cave to the actual objects without it. They consider men 'as mice in an air-pump,' fit only for their experiments; and do not consider the rest of the universe, or 'all the mighty world of eye and ear,' as worth any notice at all. This is making short, but not sure work. Truth does not lie *in vacuo,* any more than in a well. We must improve our concrete experience of persons and things into the contemplation of general rules and principles; but without being grounded in individual facts and feelings, we shall end as we began, in ignorance.

It is mentioned in a short account of the *Last Moments of Mr Fox*, that the conversation at the house

— *On Reason and Imagination* —

of Lord Holland (where he died) turning upon Mr Burke's style, that Noble Person objected to it as too gaudy and meretricious, and said that it was more profuse of flowers than fruit. On which Mr Fox observed, that though this was a common objection, it appeared to him altogether an unfounded one; that on the contrary, the flowers often concealed the fruit beneath them, and the ornaments of style were rather an hindrance than an advantage to the sentiments they were meant to set off. In confirmation of this remark, he offered to take down the book, and translate a page any where into his own plain, natural style; and by his doing so, Lord Holland was convinced that he had often missed the thought from having his attention drawn off to the dazzling imagery. Thus people continually find fault with the colours of style as incompatible with the truth of the reasoning, but without any foundation whatever. If it were a question about the figure of two triangles, and any person were to object that one triangle was green and the other yellow, and bring this to bear upon the acuteness or obtuseness of the angles, it would be obvious to remark that the colour had nothing to do with the question. But in a dispute whether two objects are coloured alike, the discovery that one is green and the other yellow is fatal. So with respect to moral truth (as distinct from mathematical), whether a thing is good or evil, depends on the quantity of passion, of feeling, of pleasure and pain connected with it, and with which we must be made acquainted in order

— ALL THAT IS WORTH REMEMBERING —

to come to a sound conclusion, and not on the inquiry, whether it is round or square. Passion, in short, is the essence, the chief ingredient in moral truth; and the warmth of passion is sure to kindle the light of imagination on the objects around it. The 'words that glow' are almost inseparable from the 'thoughts that burn.' Hence logical reason and practical truth are *disparates.* It is easy to raise an outcry against violent invectives, to talk loud against extravagance and enthusiasm, to pick a quarrel with every thing but the most calm, candid, and qualified statement of facts: but there are enormities to which no words can do adequate justice. Are we then, in order to form a complete idea of them, to omit every circumstance of aggravation, or to suppress every feeling of impatience that arises out of the details, lest we should be accused of giving way to the influence of prejudice and passion? This would be to falsify the impression altogether, to misconstrue reason, and fly in the face of nature. Suppose, for instance, that in the discussions on the Slave-Trade, a description to the life was given of the horrors of the *Middle Passage* (as it was termed), that you saw the manner in which thousands of wretches, year after year, were stowed together in the hold of a slave-ship, without air, without light, without food, without hope, so that what they suffered in reality was brought home to you in imagination, till you felt in sickness of heart as one of them, could it be said that this was a prejudging of the case, that your knowing the extent of the evil disqualified

— *On Reason and Imagination* —

you from pronouncing sentence upon it, and that your disgust and abhorrence were the effects of a heated imagination? No. Those evils that inflame the imagination and make the heart sick, ought not to leave the head cool. This is the very test and measure of the degree of the enormity, that it involuntarily staggers and appals the mind. If it were a common iniquity, if it were slight and partial, or necessary, it would not have this effect; but it very properly carries away the feelings, and (if you will) overpowers the judgment, because it is a mass of evil so monstrous and unwarranted as not to be endured, even in thought. A man on the rack does not suffer the less, because the extremity of anguish takes away his command of feeling and attention to appearances. A pang inflicted on humanity is not the less real, because it stirs up sympathy in the breast of humanity. Would you tame down the glowing language of justifiable passion into that of cold indifference, of self-complacent, sceptical reasoning, and thus take out the sting of indignation from the mind of the spectator? Not, surely, till you have removed the nuisance by the levers that strong feeling alone can set at work, and have thus taken away the pang of suffering that caused it! Or say that the question were proposed to you, whether, on some occasion, you should thrust your hand into the flames, and were coolly told that you were not at all to consider the pain and anguish it might give you, nor suffer yourself to be led away by any such idle appeals to natural sensibility, but to refer the decision to some abstract, technical ground of propriety, would you not laugh in your adviser's face? Oh! no; where your own interests are concerned, or where we are sincere in our professions of regard, the pretended distinction between sound judgment and lively imagination is quickly done away with. But I would not wish a better or more philosophical standard of morality, than that we should think and feel towards others as we should, if it were our own case. If we look for a higher standard than this, we shall not find it; but shall lose the substance for the shadow! Again, suppose an extreme or individual instance is brought forward in any general question, as that of the cargo of sick slaves that were thrown overboard as so much *live lumber* by the captain of a Guinea vessel, in the year 1775, which was one of the things that first drew the attention of the public to this nefarious traffic,* or the practice of suspending contumacious negroes in cages to have their eyes pecked out, and to be devoured alive by birds of prey—Does this form no rule, because the mischief is solitary or excessive? The rule is absolute; for we feel that nothing of the kind could take place, or be tolerated for an instant, in any system that was not rotten at the core. If such things are ever done in any circumstances with impunity, we know what must be done every day under the same sanction. It shows that there is an utter deadness to every principle of justice

---

* See *Memoirs of Granville Sharp*, by Prince Hoare, Esq.

— *On Reason and Imagination* —

or feeling of humanity; and where this is the case, we may take out our tables of abstraction, and set down what is to follow through every gradation of petty, galling vexation, and wanton, unrelenting cruelty. A state of things, where a single instance of the kind can possibly happen without exciting general consternation, ought not to exist for half an hour. The parent, hydra-headed injustice ought to be crushed at once with all its viper brood. Practices, the mention of which makes the flesh creep, and that affront the light of day, ought to be put down the instant they are known, without inquiry and without repeal.

There was an example of eloquent moral reasoning connected with this subject, given in the work just referred to, which was not the less solid and profound, because it was produced by a burst of strong personal and momentary feeling. It is what follows:—'The name of a person having been mentioned in the presence of Naimbanna (a young African chieftain), who was understood by him to have publicly asserted something very degrading to the general character of Africans, he broke out into violent and vindictive language. He was immediately reminded of the Christian duty of forgiving his enemies; upon which he answered nearly in the following words:—'If a man should rob me of my money, I can forgive him; if a man should shoot at me, or try to stab me, I can forgive him; if a man should sell me and all my family to a slave-ship, so that we should pass all the rest of our days in slavery in the West Indies,

— ALL THAT IS WORTH REMEMBERING —

I can forgive him; but' (added he, rising from his seat with much emotion) 'if a man takes away the character of the people of my country, I never can forgive him.' Being asked why he would not extend his forgiveness to those who took away the character of the people of his country, he answered: 'If a man should try to kill me, or should sell me and my family for slaves, he would do an injury to as many as he might kill or sell; but if any one takes away the character of Black people, that man injures Black people all over the world; and when he has once taken away their character, there is nothing which he may not do to Black people ever after. That man, for instance, will beat Black men, and say, *Oh, it is only a Black man, why should not I beat him?* That man will make slaves of Black people; for, when he has taken away their character, he will say, *Oh, they are only Black people, why should not I make them slaves?* That man will take away all the people of Africa if he can catch them; and if you ask him, But why do you take away all these people? he will say, *Oh! they are only Black people—they are not like White people—why should I not take them?* That is the reason why I cannot forgive the man who takes away the character of the people of my country.'—MEMOIRS OF GRANVILLE SHARP, p.369.

I conceive more real light and vital heat is thrown into the argument by this struggle of natural feeling to relieve itself from the weight of a false and injurious imputation, than would be added to it by twenty

— *On Reason and Imagination* —

volumes of tables and calculations of the *pros* and *cons* of right and wrong, of utility and inutility, in Mr Bentham's handwriting. In allusion to this celebrated person's theory of morals, I will here go a step farther, and deny that the dry calculation of consequences is the sole and unqualified test of right and wrong; for we are to take into the account (as well) the re-action of these consequences upon the mind of the individual and the community. In morals, the cultivation of a *moral sense* is not the last thing to be attended to—nay, it is the first. Almost the only unsophisticated or spirited remark that we meet with in Paley's *Moral Philosophy*, is one which is also to be found in Tucker's *Light of Nature*—namely, that in dispensing charity to common beggars we are not to consider so much the good it may do the object of it, as the harm it will do the person who refuses it. A sense of compassion is involuntarily excited by the immediate appearance of distress, and a violence and injury is done to the kindly feelings by withholding the obvious relief, the trifling pittance in our power. This is a remark, I think, worthy of the ingenious and amiable author from whom Paley borrowed it. So with respect to the atrocities committed in the Slave-Trade, it could not be set up as a doubtful plea in their favour, that the actual and intolerable sufferings inflicted on the individuals were compensated by certain advantages in a commercial and political point of view—in a moral sense they *cannot* be compensated. They hurt the public mind: they harden and sear the natural feelings. The evil is monstrous and palpable; the pretended good is remote and contingent. In morals, as in philosophy, *De non apparentibus et non existentibus eadem est ratio.* What does not touch the heart, or come home to the feelings, goes comparatively for little or nothing, A benefit that exists merely in possibility, and is judged of only by the forced dictates of the understanding, is not a set-off against an evil (say of equal magnitude in itself) that strikes upon the senses, that haunts the imagination, and lacerates the human heart. A spectacle of deliberate cruelty, that shocks every one that sees and hears of it, is not to be justified by any calculations of cold-blooded self-interest—is not to be permitted in any case. It is prejudged and self-condemned. Necessity has been therefore justly called 'the tyrant's plea.' It is no better with the mere doctrine of utility, which is the sophist's plea. Thus, for example, an infinite number of lumps of sugar put into Mr Bentham's artificial ethical scales would never weigh against the pounds of human flesh, or drops of human blood, that are sacrificed to produce them. The taste of the former on the palate is evanescent; but the others sit heavy on the soul. The one are an object to the imagination: the others only to the understanding. But man is an animal compounded both of imagination and understanding; and, in treating of what is good for man's nature, it is necessary to consider both. A calculation of the mere ultimate advantages, without regard to natural feelings and affections, may improve

— *On Reason and Imagination* —

the external face and physical comforts of society, but will leave it heartless and worthless in itself. In a word, the sympathy of the individual with the consequences of his own act is to be attended to (no less than the consequences themselves) in every sound system of morality; and this must be determined by certain natural laws of the human mind, and not by rules of logic or arithmetic.

The aspect of a moral question is to be judged of very much like the face of a country, by the projecting points, by what is striking and memorable, by that which leaves traces of itself behind, or 'casts its shadow before.' Millions of acres do not make a picture; nor the calculation of all the consequences in the world a sentiment. We must have some outstanding object for the mind, as well as the eye, to dwell on and recur to—something marked and decisive to give a tone and texture to the moral feelings. Not only is the attention thus roused and kept alive; but what is most important as to the principles of action, the desire of good or hatred of evil is powerfully excited. But all individual facts and history come under the head of what these people call *Imagination.* All full, true, and particular accounts they consider as romantic, ridiculous, vague, inflammatory. As a case in point, one of this school of thinkers declares that he was qualified to write a better History of India from having never been there than if he had, as the last might lead to local distinctions or party-prejudices; that is to say, that he could describe a country better at second-hand than from original observation, or that from having seen no one object, place, or person, he could do ampler justice to the whole. It might be maintained, much on the same principle, that an artist would paint a better likeness of a person after he was dead, from description or different sketches of the face, than from having seen the individual living man. On the contrary, I humbly conceive that the seeing half a dozen wandering Lascars in the streets of London gives one a better idea of the soul of India, that cradle of the world, and (as it were) garden of the sun, than all the charts, records, and statistical reports that can be sent over, even under the classical administration of Mr Canning. *Ex uno omnes.* One Hindoo differs more from a citizen of London than he does from all other Hindoos; and by seeing the two first, man to man, you know comparatively and essentially what they are, nation to nation. By a very few specimens you fix the great leading differences, which are nearly the same throughout. Any one thing is a better representative of its kind, than all the words and definitions in the world can be. The sum total is indeed different from the particulars; but it is not easy to guess at any general result, without some previous induction of particulars and appeal to experience.

'What can we reason, but from what we know?'

— *On Reason and Imagination* —

Again, it is quite wrong, instead of the most striking illustrations of human nature, to single out the stalest and tritest, as if they were most authentic and infallible; not considering that from the extremes you may infer the means, but you cannot from the means infer the extremes in any case. It may be said that the extreme and individual cases may be retorted upon us:—I deny it, unless it be with truth. The imagination is an *associating* principle; and has an instinctive perception when a thing belongs to a system, or is only an exception to it. For instance, the excesses committed by the victorious besiegers of a town do not attach to the nation committing them, but to the nature of that sort of warfare, and are common to both sides. They may be struck off the score of national prejudices. The cruelties exercised upon slaves, on the other hand, grow out of the relation between master and slave; and the mind intuitively revolts at them as such. The cant about the horrors of the French Revolution is mere cant—every body knows it to be so: each party would have retaliated upon the other: it was a civil war, like that for a disputed succession: the general principle of the right or wrong of the change remained untouched. Neither would these horrors have taken place, except from Prussian manifestos, and treachery within: there were none in the American, and have been none in the Spanish Revolution. The massacre of St Bartholomew arose out of the principles of that religion which exterminates with fire and sword, and keeps no faith with heretics.—If it be said that nick-names, party watch-words, bugbears, the cry of 'No Popery,' &c. are continually played off upon the imagination with the most mischievous effect, I answer that most of these bugbears and terms of vulgar abuse have arisen out of abstruse speculation or barbarous prejudice, and have seldom had their root in real facts or natural feelings. Besides, are not general topics, rules, exceptions, endlessly bandied to and fro, and balanced one against the other by the most learned disputants? Have not three-fourths of all the wars, schisms, heart-burnings in the world begun on mere points of controversy?—There are two classes whom I have found given to this kind of reasoning against the use of our senses and feelings in what concerns human nature, *viz.* knaves and fools. The last do it, because they think their own shallow dogmas settle all questions best without any farther appeal; and the first do it, because they know that the refinements of the head are more easily got rid of than the suggestions of the heart, and that a strong sense of injustice, excited by a particular case in all its aggravations, tells more against them than all the distinctions of the jurists. Facts, concrete existences, are stubborn things, and are not so soon tampered with or turned about to any point we please, as mere names and abstractions. Of these last it may be said,

'A breath can *mar* them, as a breath has made:'

— *On Reason and Imagination* —

and they are liable to be puffed away by every wind of doctrine, or baffled by every plea of convenience. I wonder that Rousseau gave into this cant about the want of soundness in rhetorical and imaginative reasoning; and was so fond of this subject, as to make an abridgment of Plato's rhapsodies upon it, by which he was led to expel poets from his commonwealth. Thus two of the most flowery writers are those who have exacted the greatest severity of style from others. Rousseau was too ambitious of an exceedingly technical and scientific mode of reasoning, scarcely attainable in the mixed questions of human life, (as may be seen in his SOCIAL CONTRACT—a work of great ability, but extreme formality of structure) and it is probable he was led into this error in seeking to overcome his too great warmth of natural temperament and a tendency to indulge merely the impulses of passion. Burke, who was a man of fine imagination, had the good sense (without any of this false modesty) to defend the moral uses of the imagination, and is himself one of the grossest instances of its abuse.

It is not merely the fashion among philosophers—the poets also have got into a way of scouting individuality as beneath the sublimity of their pretensions, and the universality of their genius. The philosophers have become mere logicians, and their rivals mere rhetoricians; for as these last must float on the surface, and are not allowed to be harsh and crabbed and recondite like the others, by leaving out the individual, they become common-place. They cannot reason, and they must declaim. Modern tragedy, in particular, is no longer like a vessel making the voyage of life, and tossed about by the winds and waves of passion, but is converted into a handsomely-constructed steam-boat, that is moved by the sole expansive power of words. Lord Byron has launched several of these ventures lately (if ventures they may be called) and may continue in the same strain as long as he pleases. 'We have not now a number of *dramatis personae* affected by particular incidents and speaking according to their feelings, or as the occasion suggests, but each mounting the rostrum, and delivering his opinion on fate, fortune, and the entire consummation of things. The individual is not of sufficient importance to occupy his own thoughts or the thoughts of others. The poet fills his page with *grandes pensées.* He covers the face of nature with the beauty of his sentiments and the brilliancy of his paradoxes. We have the subtleties of the head, instead of the workings of the heart, and possible justifications instead of the actual motives of conduct. This all seems to proceed on a false estimate of individual nature and the value of human life. We have been so used to count by millions of late, that we think the units that compose them nothing; and are so prone to trace remote principles, that we neglect the immediate results. As an instance of the opposite style of dramatic dialogue, in which the persons speak for themselves, and to one another, I will give, by way of illustration, a passage

— *On Reason and Imagination* —

from an old tragedy, in which a brother has just caused his sister to be put to a violent death.

Bosola. Fix your eye here.
Ferdinand. Constantly.
Bosola. Do you not weep?
  Other sins only speak; murther shrieks out:
  The element of water moistens the earth;
  But blood flies upwards, and bedews the heavens.
Ferdinand. Cover her face: mine eyes dazzle; she died young.
Bosola. I think not so: her infelicity
  Seem'd to have years too many.
Ferdinand. She and I were twins:
  And should I die this instant, I had lived
  Her time to a minute.
    Duchess of Malfi, Act IV, Scene 2.

How fine is the constancy with which he first fixes his eye on the dead body, with a forced courage, and then, as his resolution wavers, how natural is his turning his face away, and the reflection that strikes him on her youth and beauty and untimely death, and the thought that they were twins, and his measuring his life by hers up to the present period, as if all that was to come of it were nothing! Now, I would fain ask whether there is not in this contemplation of the interval that separates the beginning from the end of life, of a life too so varied from good to ill, and of the pitiable termination of which the person speaking has been the wilful and guilty cause, enough to 'give the mind pause?'

— ALL THAT IS WORTH REMEMBERING —

Is not that revelation as it were of the whole extent of our being which is made by the flashes of passion and stroke of calamity, a subject sufficiently staggering to have place in legitimate tragedy? Are not the struggles of the will with untoward events and the adverse passions of others as interesting and instructive in the representation as reflections on the mutability of fortune or inevitableness of destiny, or on the passions of men in general? The tragic muse does not merely utter muffled sounds: but we see the paleness on the cheek, and the life-blood gushing from the heart! The interest we take in our own lives, in our successes or disappointments, and the *home* feelings that arise out of these, when well described, are the clearest and truest mirror in which we can see the image of human nature. For in this sense each man is a microcosm. What he is, the rest are—whatever his joys and sorrows are composed of, theirs are the same—no more, no less.

'One touch of nature makes the whole world kin.'

But it must be the genuine touch of nature, not the outward flourishes and varnish of art. The spouting, oracular, didactic figure of the poet no more answers to the living man, than the lay-figure of the painter does. We may well say to such a one,

> 'Thou hast no speculation in those eyes
> That thou dost glare with: thy bones are marrowless,
> Thy blood is cold!'

— *On Reason and Imagination* —

Man is (so to speak) an endless and infinitely varied repetition: and if we know what one man feels, we so far know what a thousand feel in the sanctuary of their being. Our feeling of general humanity is at once an aggregate of a thousand different truths, and it is also the same truth a thousand times told. As is our perception of this original truth, the root of our imagination, so will the force and richness of the general impression proceeding from it be. The boundary of our sympathy is a circle which enlarges itself according to its propulsion from the centre—the heart. If we are imbued with a deep sense of individual weal or woe, we shall be awe-struck at the idea of humanity in general. If we know little of it but its abstract and common properties, without their particular application, their force or degrees, we shall care just as little as we know either about the whole or the individuals. If we understand the texture and vital feeling, we then can fill up the outline, but we cannot supply the former from having the latter given. Moral and poetical truth is like expression in a picture—the one is not to be attained by smearing over a large canvas, nor the other by bestriding a vague topic. In such matters, the most pompous sciolists are accordingly found to be the greatest contemners of human life. But I defy any great tragic writer to despise that nature which he understands, or that heart which he has probed, with all its rich bleeding materials of joy and sorrow. The subject may not be a source of much triumph to him, from its alternate light and shade, but

— ALL THAT IS WORTH REMEMBERING —

it can never become one of supercilious indifference. He must feel a strong reflex interest in it, corresponding to that which he has depicted in the characters of others. Indeed, the object and end of playing, 'both at the first and now, is to hold the mirror up to nature,' to enable us to feel for others as for ourselves, or to embody a distinct interest out of ourselves by the force of imagination and passion. This is summed up in the wish of the poet—

'To feel what others are, and know myself a man.'

If it does not do this, it loses both its dignity and its proper use.

– On the Spirit of Monarchy –

> First published in *The Liberal*, January 1823, not reprinted during Hazlitt's lifetime; reproduced from *The Liberal*. This is one of Hazlitt's most engaged attacks on the institution of monarch, the highlight of which is a satirical description of the coronation of George IV ('he staggers and reels under the weight of royal pomp').

'Strip it of its externals, and what is it but *a jest?*'
  Charade on the word MAJESTY.

'As for politics, I think poets are *Tories* by nature, supposing them to be by nature poets. The love of an individual person or family, that has worn a crown for many successions, is an inclination greatly adapted to the fanciful tribe. On the other hand, mathematicians, abstract reasoners, of no manner of attachment to persons, at least to the visible part of them, but prodigiously devoted to the ideas of virtue, liberty, and so forth, are generally *Whigs.* It happens agreeably enough to this maxim, that the Whigs are friends to that wise, plodding, unpoetical people, the Dutch.'—*Shenstone's Letters,* 1746.

T he Spirit of Monarchy then is nothing but the craving in the human mind after the Sensible and the One. It is not so much a matter of state-necessity or policy, as a natural infirmity, a disease, a false appetite in the popular feeling, which must be gratified. Man is an individual animal with narrow faculties, but infinite desires, which he is anxious to concentrate in some one object within the grasp of his imagination, and where, if he cannot be all that he wishes himself, he may at least contemplate his own pride, vanity, and passions, displayed in their most extravagant dimensions in a being no bigger and no better than himself. Each individual would (were it in his power) be a king, a god: but as he cannot, the next best thing is to see this reflex image of his self-love, the darling passion of his breast, realized, embodied out of himself in the first object he can lay his hands on for the purpose. The slave admires the tyrant, because the last *is,* what the first *would be.* He surveys himself all over in the glass of royalty. The swelling, bloated self-importance of the one is the very counterpart and ultimate goal of the abject servility of the other. But both hate mankind for the same reason, because a respect for humanity is a diversion to their inordinate self-love, and the idea of the general good is a check to the gross intemperance of passion. The worthlessness of the object does not diminish but irritate the propensity to admire. It serves to pamper our imagination equally, and does not provoke our envy. All we want is to aggrandize our own vain-glory at second-hand; and the less of real superiority or excellence there is in the person we fix upon as our proxy in this dramatic exhibition, the more easily

— *On the Spirit of Monarchy* —

can we change places with him, and fancy ourselves as good as he. Nay, the descent favours the rise; and we heap our tribute of applause the higher, in proportion as it is a free gift. An idol is not the worse for being of coarse materials: a king should be a common-place man. Otherwise, he is superior in his own nature, and not dependent on our bounty or caprice. Man is a poetical animal, and delights in fiction. We like to have scope for the exercise of our mere will. We make kings of men, and Gods of stocks and stones: we are not jealous of the creatures of our own hands. We only want a peg or loop to hang our idle fancies on, a puppet to dress up, a lay-figure to paint from. It is 'THING Ferdinand, and not KING Ferdinand,' as it was wisely and wittily observed. We ask only for the stage effect; we do not go behind the scenes, or it would go hard with many of our prejudices! We see the symbols of majesty, we enjoy the pomp, we crouch before the power, we walk in the procession, and make part of the pageant, and we say in our secret hearts, there is nothing but accident that prevents us from being at the head of it. There is something in the mock-sublimity of thrones, wonderfully congenial to the human mind. Every man feels that he could sit there; every man feels that he could look big there; every man feels that he could bow there; every man feels that he could play the monarch there. The transition is so easy, and so delightful! The imagination keeps pace with royal state,

'And by the vision splendid
Is on its way attended.'

The madman in Hogarth who fancies himself a king, is not a solitary instance of this species of hallucination. Almost every true and loyal subject holds such a barren sceptre in his hand; and the meanest of the rabble, as he runs by the monarch's side, has wit enough to think—'There goes my *royal* self!' From the most absolute despot to the lowest slave there is but one step (no, not one) in point of real merit. As far as truth or reason is concerned, they might change situations to-morrow—nay, they constantly do so without the smallest loss or benefit to mankind! Tyranny, in a word, is a farce got up for the entertainment of poor human nature; and it might pass very well, if it did not so often turn into a tragedy.

We once heard a celebrated and elegant historian and a hearty Whig declare, he liked a king like George III better than such a one as Buonaparte; because, in the former case, there was nothing to overawe the imagination but birth and situation; whereas he could not so easily brook the double superiority of the other, mental as well as adventitious. So does the spirit of independence and the levelling pride of intellect join in with the servile rage of the vulgar! This is the advantage which an hereditary has over an elective monarchy: for there is no end of the dispute about precedence while merit is supposed to determine it, each man laying claim to

— *On the Spirit of Monarchy* —

this in his own person; so that there is no other way to set aside all controversy and heart-burnings, but by precluding moral and intellectual qualifications altogether, and referring the choice to accident, and giving the preference to a nonentity. 'A good king,' says Swift, 'should be, in all other respects, a mere cypher.'

It has been remarked, as a peculiarity in modern criticism, that the courtly and loyal make a point of crying up Mr Young, as an actor, and equally running down Mr Kean; and it has been conjectured in consequence that Mr Kean was a *radical*. Truly, he is not a radical politician; but what is as bad, he is a radical actor. He savours too much of the reality. He is not a mock-tragedian, an automaton player—he is something besides his paraphernalia. He has 'that within which passes shew.' There is not a particle of affinity between him and the patrons of the court-writers. Mr Young, on the contrary, is the very thing—all assumption and strut and measured pomp, full of self-importance, void of truth and nature, the mask of the characters he takes; a pasteboard figure, a stiff piece of wax-work. He fills the throne of tragedy, not like an upstart or usurper, but as a matter of course, decked out in his plumes of feathers, and robes of state, stuck into a posture, and repeating certain words by rote. Mr Kean has a heart in his bosom, beating with human passion (a thing for the great 'to fear, not to delight in!') he is a living man, and not an artificial one. How should those, who look to the surface, and never probe deeper, endure him?

— ALL THAT IS WORTH REMEMBERING —

He is the antithesis of a court actor. It is the object there to suppress and varnish over the feelings, not to give way to them. His *overt* manner must shock them, and be thought a breach of all decorum. They are in dread of his fiery humours, of coming near his Voltaic Battery—they chuse rather to be roused gently from their self-complacent apathy by the application of Metallic Tractors. They dare not trust their delicate nerves within the estuary of the passions, but would slumber out their torpid existence in a calm, a Dead Sea—the air of which extinguishes life and motion!

Would it not be hard upon a little girl, who is busy in dressing up a favourite doll, to pull it in pieces before her face in order to shew her the bits of wood, the wool, and rags it is composed of? So it would be hard upon that great baby, the world, to take any of its idols to pieces, and shew that they are nothing but painted wood. Neither of them would thank you, but consider the offer as an insult. The little girl knows as well as you do that her doll is a cheat; but she shuts her eyes to it, for she finds her account in keeping up the deception. Her doll is her pretty little self. In its glazed eyes, its cherry cheeks, its flaxen locks, its finery and its baby-house, she has a fairy vision of her own future charms, her future triumphs, a thousand hearts led captive, and an establishment for life. Harmless illusion! that can create something out of nothing, can make that which is good for nothing in itself so fine in appearance, and clothe a shapeless piece of deal-board

— *On the Spirit of Monarchy* —

with the attributes of a divinity! But the great world has been doing little else but playing at *make-believe* all its life-time. For several thousand years its chief rage was to paint larger pieces of wood and smear them with gore and call them gods and offer victims to them —slaughtered hecatombs, the fat of goats and oxen, or human sacrifices—shewing in this its love of shew, of cruelty, and imposture; and woe to him who should 'peep through the blanket of the dark to cry, *Hold, hold*'—*Great is Diana of the Ephesians,* was the answer in all ages. It was in vain to represent to them—'Your gods have eyes but they see not, ears but they hear not, neither do they understand'—the more stupid, brutish, helpless, and contemptible they were, the more furious, bigotted, and implacable were their votaries in their behalf.* The more absurd the fiction, the louder was the noise made to hide it—the more mischievous its tendency, the more did it excite all the phrensy of the passions. Superstition nursed, with peculiar zeal, her ricketty, deformed, and preposterous offspring. She passed by the nobler races of animals even, to pay divine honours to the odious and unclean—she took toads and serpents, cats, rats, dogs, crocodiles, goats and monkeys, and hugged them to her bosom, and dandled them into deities, and set up

---

* 'Of whatsoe'er descent his godhead be,
Stock, stone, or other homely pedigree,
In his defence his servants are as bold
As if he had been made of beaten gold.'—DRYDEN

altars to them, and drenched the earth with tears and blood in their defence; and those who did not believe in them were cursed, and were forbidden the use of bread, of fire, and water, and to worship them was piety, and their images were held sacred, and their race became gods in perpetuity and by divine right. To touch them, was sacrilege: to kill them, death, even in your own defence. If they stung you, you must die: if they infested the land with their numbers and their pollutions, there was no remedy. The nuisance was intolerable, impassive, immortal. Fear, religious horror, disgust, hatred, heightened the flame of bigotry and intolerance. There was nothing so odious or contemptible but it found a sanctuary in the more odious and contemptible perversity of human nature. The barbarous gods of antiquity reigned *in contempt of their worshippers*!

This game was carried on through all the first ages of the world, and is still kept up in many parts of it; and it is impossible to describe the wars, massacres, horrors, miseries and crimes, to which it gave colour, sanctity, and sway. The idea of a god, beneficent and just, the invisible maker of all things, was abhorrent to their gross, material notions. No, they must have gods of their own making, that they could see and handle, that they knew to be nothing in themselves but senseless images, and these they daubed over with the gaudy emblems of their own pride and passions, and these they lauded to the skies, and grew fierce, obscene,

— On the Spirit of Monarchy —

frantic before them, as the representatives of their sordid ignorance and barbaric vices. TRUTH, GOOD, were idle names to them, without a meaning. They must have a lie, a palpable, pernicious lie, to pamper their crude, unhallowed conceptions with, and to exercise the untameable fierceness of their wills. The Jews were the only people of antiquity who were withheld from running headlong into this abomination; yet so strong was the propensity in them (from inherent frailty as well as neighbouring example) that it could only be curbed and kept back by the hands of Omnipotence.* At length, reason prevailed over imagination so far, that these brute idols and their altars were overturned: it was thought too much to set up stocks and stones, Golden Calves and Brazen Serpents, as *bona fide* gods and goddesses, which men were to fall down and worship at their peril—and Pope long after summed up the merits of the whole mythologic tribe in a handsome distich—

> 'Gods partial, changeful, passionate, unjust,
> Whose attributes were rage, revenge, or lust.'

It was thought a bold stride to divert the course of our imagination, the overflowings of our enthusiasm, our love of the mighty and the marvellous, from the

---

* They *would* have a king in spite of the devil. The image-worship of the Papists is a batch of the same leaven. The apishness of man's nature would not let even the Christian Religion escape.

dead to the living *subject*, and there we stick. We have got living idols, instead of dead ones; and we fancy that they are real, and put faith in them accordingly. Oh, Reason! when will thy long minority expire? It is not now the fashion to make Gods of wood and stone and brass, but we make kings of common men, and are proud of our own handiwork. We take a child from his birth, and we agree, when he grows up to be a man, to heap the highest honours of the state upon him, and to pay the most devoted homage to his will. Is there any thing in the person, 'any mark, any likelihood,' to warrant this sovereign awe and dread? No: he may be little better than an ideot, little short of a madman, and yet he is no less qualified for king.* If he can contrive

---

*'In fact, the argument drawn from the supposed incapacity of the people against a representative Government, comes with the worst grace in the world from the patrons and admirers of hereditary government. Surely, if government were a thing requiring the utmost stretch of genius, wisdom, and virtue to carry it on, the office of King would never even have been dreamt of as hereditary, any more than that of poet, painter, or philosopher. It is easy here 'for the Son to tread in the Sire's steady steps.' It requires nothing but the will to do it. Extraordinary talents are not once looked for. Nay, a person, who would never have risen by natural abilities to the situation of churchwarden or parish beadle, succeeds by unquestionable right to the possession of a throne, and wields the energies of an empire, or decides the fate of the world with the smallest possible share of human understanding. The line of distinction which separates the regal purple from the slabbering-bib is sometimes fine indeed; as we see in the case of the two Ferdinands. Any one above the rank of an ideot is supposed capable of exercising the highest functions of royal state. Yet these are the persons who talk of the people as a swinish multitude, and taunt them with their want of refinement and philosophy.'—*Yellow Dwarf*, p.84.

— *On the Spirit of Monarchy* —

to pass the College of Physicians, the Heralds' College dub him divine. Can we make any given individual taller or stronger or wiser than other men, or different in any respect from what nature intended him to be? No; but we can make a king of him. We cannot add a cubit to the stature, or instil a virtue into the minds of monarchs—but we can put a sceptre into their hands, a crown upon their heads, we can set them on an eminence, we can surround them with circumstance, we can aggrandise them with power, we can pamper their appetites, we can pander to their wills. We can do every thing to exalt them in external rank and station—nothing to lift them one step higher in the scale of moral or intellectual excellence. Education does not give capacity or temper; and the education of kings is not especially directed to useful knowledge or liberal sentiment. What then is the state of the case? The highest respect of the community and of every individual in it is paid and is due of right there, where perhaps not an idea can take root, or a single virtue be engrafted. Is not this to erect a standard of esteem directly opposite to that of mind and morals? The lawful monarch may be the best or the worst man in his dominions, he may be the wisest or the weakest, the wittiest or the stupidest: still he is equally entitled to our homage as king, for it is the place and power we bow to, and not the man. He may be a sublimation of all the vices and diseases of the human heart; yet we are not to say so, we dare not even think so. 'Fear God, and honour the King,' is equally a maxim at all times and seasons. The personal character of the king has nothing to do with the question. Thus the extrinsic is set up over the intrinsic by authority: wealth and interest lend their countenance to gilded vice and infamy on principle, and outward shew and advantages become the symbols and the standard of respect in despite of useful qualities or well-directed efforts through all ranks and gradations of society. 'From the crown of the head to the sole of the foot there is no soundness left.' The whole style of moral thinking, feeling, acting, is in a false tone—is hollow, spurious, meretricious. Virtue, says Montesquieu, is the principle of republics; honour of a monarchy. But it is 'honour dishonourable, sin-bred'—it is the honour of trucking a principle for a place, of exchanging our honest convictions for a ribbon or a garter. The business of life is a scramble for unmerited precedence. Is not the highest respect entailed, the highest station filled without any possible proofs or pretensions to public spirit or public principle? Shall not the next places to it be secured by the sacrifice of them? It is the order of the day, the understood etiquette of courts and kingdoms. For the servants of the crown to presume on merit, when the crown itself is held as an heirloom by prescription, is a kind of *lèse majesté,* an indirect attainder of the title to the succession. Are not all eyes turned to the sun of court-favour? Who would not then reflect its smile by the performance of any acts which can avail in the eye of the great, and by the surrender of any virtue,

— *On the Spirit of Monarchy* —

which attracts neither notice nor applause? The stream of corruption begins at the fountainhead of court-influence. The sympathy of mankind is that on which all strong feeling and opinion floats; and this sets in full in every absolute monarchy to the side of tinsel shew and iron-handed power, in contempt and defiance of right and wrong. The right and the wrong are of little consequence, compared to the *in* and the *out*. The distinction between Whig and Tory is merely nominal: neither have their country one bit at heart. Phaw! we had forgot—Our British monarchy is a mixed, and the only perfect form of government; and therefore what is here said cannot properly apply to it. But MIGHT BEFORE RIGHT is the motto blazoned on the front of unimpaired and undivided Sovereignty!—

A court is the centre of fashion; and no less so, for being the sink of luxury and vice—

—'Of outward shew
Elaborate, of inward less exact.'

The goods of fortune, the baits of power, the indulgences of vanity, may be accumulated without end, and the taste for them increases as it is gratified: the love of virtue, the pursuit of truth, grow stale and dull in the dissipation of a court. Virtue is thought crabbed and morose, knowledge pedantic, while every sense is pampered, and every folly tolerated. Every thing tends naturally to personal aggrandisement and unrestrained self-will. It is easier for monarchs as well as other men 'to tread the primrose path of dalliance' than 'to scale the steep and thorny road to heaven.' The vices, when they have leave from power and authority, go greater lengths than the virtues; example justifies almost every excess, and 'nice customs curtsy to great kings.' What chance is there that monarchs should not yield to the temptations of gallantry there, where youth and beauty are as wax? What female heart can indeed withstand the attractions of a throne—the smile that melts all hearts, the air that awes rebellion, the frown that kings dread, the hand that scatters fairy wealth, that bestows titles, places, honour, power, the breast on which the star glitters, the head circled with a diadem, whose dress dazzles with its richness and its taste, who has nations at his command, senates at his control, 'in form and motion so express and admirable, in action how like an angel, in apprehension how like a god; the beauty of the world, the paragon of animals!' The power of resistance is so much the less, where fashion extends impunity to the frail offender, and screens the loss of character.

> 'Vice is undone, if she forgets her birth,
> And stoops from angels to the dregs of earth;
> But 'tis the fall degrades her to a whore:
> Let greatness own her, and she's mean no more.
> Her birth, her beauty, crowds and courts confess,
> Chaste matrons praise her, and grave bishops bless.

— *On the Spirit of Monarchy* —

In golden chains the willing world she draws,
And hers the Gospel is, and hers the laws.'*

The air of a court is not assuredly that which is most favourable to the practice of self-denial and strict morality. We increase the temptations of wealth, of power, and pleasure a thousandfold, while we can give no additional force to the antagonist principles of reason, disinterested integrity and goodness of heart. Is it to be wondered at that courts and palaces have produced so many monsters of avarice, cruelty, and lust? The adept in voluptuousness is not likely to be a proportionable proficient in humanity. To feed on plate or be clothed in

---

*A lady of quality abroad, in allusion to the gallantries of the reigning Prince, being told, 'I suppose it will be your turn next?' said, 'No, I hope not; for you know it is impossible to refuse!' What a satire on the court and fashionables! If this be true, female virtue in the blaze of royalty is no more than the moth in the candle, or ice in the sun's ray. What will the great themselves say to it, in whom at this rate,
— 'the same luck holds,
They all are subjects, courtiers, and cuckolds!'
Out upon it! We'll not believe it. Alas! poor virtue, what is to become of the very idea of it, if we are to be told that every man within the precincts of a palace is an *hypothetical* cuckold, or holds his wife's virtue in trust for the Prince? We entertain no doubt that many ladies of quality have resisted the importunities of a throne, and that many more would do so in private life, if they had the desired opportunity: nay, we have been assured by several that a king would no more be able to prevail with them than any other man! If however there is any foundation for the above insinuation, it throws no small light on the Spirit of Monarchy, which by the supposition implies in it the *virtual* surrender of the whole sex at discretion; and at the same time accounts perhaps for the indifference shewn by some monarchs in availing themselves of so mechanical a privilege.

purple, is not to feel for the hungry and the naked. He who has the greatest power put into his hands, will only become more impatient of any restraint in the use of it. To have the welfare and the lives of millions placed at our disposal, is a sort of warrant, a challenge to squander them without mercy. An arbitrary monarch set over the heads of his fellows does not identify himself with them, or learn to comprehend their rights or sympathise with their interests, but looks down upon them as of a different species from himself, as insects crawling on the face of the earth, that he may trample on at his pleasure, or if he spares them, it is an act of royal grace—he is besotted with power, blinded with prerogative, an alien to his nature, a traitor to his trust, and instead of being the organ of public feeling and public opinion, is an excrescence and an anomaly in the state, a bloated mass of morbid humours and proud flesh! A constitutional king, on the other hand, is a servant of the public, a representative of the people's wants and wishes, dispensing justice and mercy according to law. Such a monarch is the King of England! Such was his late, and such is his present Majesty George the IVth!—

Let us take the Spirit of Monarchy in its highest state of exaltation, in the moment of its proudest triumph—a Coronation-day. We now see it in our mind's eye; the preparation of weeks—the expectation of months—the seats, the privileged places, are occupied in the obscurity of night, and in silence—the day dawns slowly, big with the hope of Caesar and of

— *On the Spirit of Monarchy* —

Rome—the golden censers are set in order, the tables groan with splendour and with luxury—within the inner space the rows of peeresses are set, and revealed to the eye decked out in ostrich feathers and pearls, like beds of lilies sparkling with a thousand dew-drops—the marshals and the heralds are in motion—the full organ, majestic, peals forth the Coronation Anthem—every thing is ready—and all at once the Majesty of kingdoms bursts upon the astonished sight—his person is swelled out with all the gorgeousness of dress, and swathed in bales of silk and golden tissues—the bow with which he greets the assembled multitude, and the representatives of foreign kings, is the climax of conscious dignity, bending gracefully on its own bosom, and instantly thrown back into the sightless air, as if asking no recognition in return—the oath of mutual fealty between him and his people is taken—the fairest flowers of female beauty precede the Sovereign, scattering roses; the sons of princes page his heels, holding up the robes of crimson and ermine—he staggers and reels under the weight of royal pomp, and of a nation's eyes; and thus the pageant is launched into the open day, dazzling the sun, whose beams seem beaten back by the sun of royalty—there were the warrior, the statesman, and the mitred head—there was Prince Leopold, like a panther in its dark glossy pride, and Castlereagh, clad in triumphant smiles and snowy satin, unstained with his own blood—the loud trumpet brays, the cannon roars, the spires are mad with music, the stones in the street are startled at the presence of a king:—the crowd press on, the metropolis heaves like a sea in restless motion, the air is thick with loyalty's quick pants in its monarch's arms—all eyes drink up the sight, all tongues reverberate the sound—

> 'A present deity they shout around,
> A present deity the vaulted roofs rebound!'

What does it all amount to? A shew—a theatrical spectacle! What does it prove? That a king is crowned, that a king is dead! What is the moral to be drawn from it, that is likely to sink into the heart of a nation? That greatness consists in finery, and that supreme merit is the dower of birth and fortune! It is a form, a ceremony to which each successor to the throne is entitled in his turn as a matter of right. Does it depend on the inheritance of virtue, on the acquisition of knowledge in the new monarch, whether he shall be thus exalted in the eyes of the people? No:—to say so is not only an offence in manners, but a violation of the laws. The king reigns in contempt of any such pragmatical distinctions. They are set aside, proscribed, treasonable, as it relates to the august person of the monarch; what is likely to become of them in the minds of the people? A Coronation overlays and drowns all such considerations for a generation to come, and so far it serves its purpose well. It debauches the understandings of the people, and makes them the slaves of sense

— *On the Spirit of Monarchy* —

and show. It laughs to scorn and tramples upon every other claim to distinction or respect. Is the chief person in the pageant a tyrant? It does not lessen, but aggrandise him to the imagination. Is he the king of a free people? We make up in love and loyalty what we want in fear. Is he young? He borrows understanding and experience from the learning and tried wisdom of councils and parliaments. Is he old? He leans upon the youth and beauty that attend his triumph. Is he weak? Armies support him with their myriads. Is he diseased? What is health to a staff of physicians? Does he die? The truth is out, and he is then—nothing!

There is a cant among court-sycophants of calling all those who are opposed to them, 'the *rabble*,' '*fellows*,' '*miscreants*' &c. This shews the grossness of their ideas of all true merit, and the false standard of rank and power by which they measure every thing; like footmen, who suppose their masters must be gentlemen, and that the rest of the world are low people. Whatever is opposed to power, they think despicable; whatever suffers oppression, they think deserves it. They are ever ready to side with the strong, to insult and trample on the weak. This is with us a pitiful fashion of thinking. They are not of the mind of Pope, who was so full of the opposite conviction, that he has even written a bad couplet to express it:—

> 'Worth makes the man, and want of it the fellow:
> The rest is all but leather and prunella.'

Those lines in Cowper also must sound very puerile or old-fashioned to courtly ears:—

> 'The only amaranthine flower on earth
> Is virtue; the only lasting treasure, truth.'

To this sentiment, however, we subscribe our hearts and hands. There is nothing truly liberal but that which postpones its own claims to those of propriety—or great, but that which looks out of itself to others. All power is but an unabated nuisance, a barbarous assumption, an aggravated injustice, that is not directed to the common good: all grandeur that has not something corresponding to it in personal merit and heroic acts, is a deliberate burlesque, and an insult on common sense and human nature. That which is true, the understanding ratifies: that which is good, the heart owns: all other claims are spurious, vitiated, mischievous, false—fit only for those who are sunk below contempt, or raised above opinion. We hold in scorn all *right-lined* pretensions but those of rectitude. If there is offence in this, we are ready to abide by it. If there is shame, we take it to ourselves: and we hope and hold that the time will come, when all other idols but those which represent pure truth and real good, will be looked upon with the same feelings of pity and wonder that we now look back to the images of Thor and Woden!

Really, that men born to a throne (limited or unlimited) should employ the brief span of their exist-

— *On the Spirit of Monarchy* —

ence here in doing all the mischief in their power, in levying cruel wars and undermining the liberties of the world, to prove to themselves and others that their pride and passions are of more consequence than the welfare of mankind at large, would seem a little astonishing, but that the fact is so. It is not our business to preach lectures to monarchs, but if we were at all disposed to attempt the ungracious task, we should do it in the words of an author who often addressed the ear of monarchs.

'A man may read a sermon,' says Jeremy Taylor, 'the best and most passionate that ever man preached, if he shall but enter into the sepulchres of kings. In the same Escurial where the Spanish princes live in greatness and power, and decree war or peace, they have wisely placed a cemetery where their ashes and their glory shall sleep till time shall be no more: and where *our* kings have been crowned, their ancestors lie interred, and they must walk over their grandsire's head to take his crown. There is an acre sown with royal seed, the copy of the greatest change from rich to naked, from ceiled roofs to arched coffins, from living like gods to die like men. There is enough to cool the flames of lust, to abate the height of pride, to appease the itch of covetous desires, to sully and dash out the dissembling colours of a lustful, artificial, and imaginary beauty. There the warlike and the peaceful, the fortunate and the miserable, the beloved and the despised princes mingle their dust, and pay down their symbol of mortality, and tell all the world, that when we die our ashes shall be equal to kings, and our accounts shall be easier, and our pains for our crimes shall be less. To my apprehension, it is a sad record which is left by Athenaeus concerning Ninus, the great Assyrian monarch, whose life and death is summed up in these words: 'Ninus, the Assyrian, had an ocean of gold, and other riches more than the sand in the Caspian sea; he never saw the stars, and perhaps he never desired it; he never stirred up the holy fire among the Magi; nor touched his God with the sacred rod, according to the laws; he never offered sacrifice, nor worshipped the Deity, nor administered justice, nor spake to the people, nor numbered them; but he was most valiant to eat and drink, and having mingled his wines, he threw the rest upon the stones. This man is dead: behold his sepulchre, and now hear where Ninus is. *Sometime I was Ninus, and drew the breath of a living man, but now am nothing but clay. I have nothing but what I did eat, and what I served to myself in lust is all my portion: the wealth with which I was blest, my enemies meeting together shall carry away, as the mad Thyades carry a raw goat. I am gone to Hell; and when I went thither, I carried neither gold nor horse, nor a silver chariot. I that wore a mitre, am now a little heap of dust!*'—TAYLOR'S HOLY LIVING AND DYING.

– Sir Walter Scott –

First published *New Monthly Magazine*, April 1824, reprinted in *The Spirit of the Age* (1825); reproduced here from the second edition of *The Spirit of the Age* (1825). In earlier years Hazlitt aspired to be a portraitist; he fulfilled that ambition in the essays on eminent contemporaries published as *The Spirit of the Age*, of which this is one of the best. Hazlitt detested Scott's conservatism as much as he admired the Waverley novels, and so declined to meet their author even though he had at least two opportunities to do so (in Scotland and Paris). Scott's reactionary politics were, in Hazlitt's eyes, unforgiveable, and prompted addition of the essay's concluding section (see pp.127–9) which was not part of the text when it first appeared in the *New Monthly Magazine*.

Sir Walter Scott is undoubtedly the most popular writer of the age—the 'lord of the ascendant' for the time being. He is just half what the human intellect is capable of being: if you take the universe, and divide it into two parts, he knows all that it *has been*; all that it *is to be* is nothing to him. His is a mind brooding over antiquity—scorning 'the present ignorant time.' He is 'laudator temporis acti'—a '*prophesier* of things past.'

— ALL THAT IS WORTH REMEMBERING —

The old world is to him a crowded map; the new one a dull, hateful blank. He dotes on all well-authenticated superstitions; he shudders at the shadow of innovation. His retentiveness of memory, his accumulated weight of interested prejudice or romantic association have overlaid his other faculties. The cells of his memory are vast, various, full even to bursting with life and motion; his speculative understanding is empty, flaccid, poor, and dead. His mind receives and treasures up every thing brought to it by tradition or custom—it does not project itself beyond this into the world unknown, but mechanically shrinks back as from the edge of a prejudice. The land of pure reason is to his apprehension like Van Dieman's Land;—barren, miserable, distant, a place of exile, the dreary abode of savages, convicts, and adventurers. Sir Walter would make a bad hand of a description of the Millennium, unless he could lay the scene in Scotland five hundred years ago, and then he would want facts and worm-eaten parchments to support his drooping style. Our historical novelist firmly thinks that nothing *is* but what *has been*—that the moral world stands still, as the material one was supposed to do of old—and that we can never get beyond the point where we actually are without utter destruction, though every thing changes and will change from what it was three hundred years ago to what it is now,—from what it is now to all that the bigoted admirer of the good old times most dreads and hates!

— *Sir Walter Scott* —

It is long since we read, and long since we thought of our author's poetry. It would probably have gone out of date with the immediate occasion, even if he himself had not contrived to banish it from our recollection. It is not to be denied that it had great merit, both of an obvious and intrinsic kind. It abounded in vivid descriptions, in spirited action, in smooth and flowing versification. But it wanted *character*. It was 'poetry of no mark or likelihood.' It slid out of the mind as soon as read, like a river; and would have been forgotten, but that the public curiosity was fed with ever new supplies from the same teeming liquid source. It is not every man that can write six quarto volumes in verse, that are caught up with avidity, even by fastidious judges. But what a difference between *their* popularity and that of the Scotch Novels! It is true, the public read and admired the *Lay of the Last Minstrel*, *Marmion*, and so on, and each individual was contented to read and admire because the public did so: but with regard to the prose-works of the same (supposed) author, it is quite *another-guess* sort of thing. Here every one stands forward to applaud on his own ground, would be thought to go before the public opinion, is eager to extol his favourite characters louder, to understand them better than every body else, and has his own scale of comparative excellence for each work, supported by nothing but his own enthusiastic and fearless convictions. It must be amusing to the Author of Waverley to hear his readers and admirers (and are not these the

— ALL THAT IS WORTH REMEMBERING —

same thing?*) quarrelling which of his novels is the best, opposing character to character, quoting passage against passage, striving to surpass each other in the extravagance of their encomiums, and yet unable to settle the precedence, or to do the author's writings justice—so various, so equal, so transcendant are their merits! His volumes of poetry were received as fashionable and well-dressed acquaintances: we are ready to tear the others in pieces as old friends. There was something meretricious in Sir Walter's ballad-rhymes; and like those who keep opera *figurantes*, we were willing to have our admiration shared, and our taste confirmed by the town: but the Novels are like the betrothed of our hearts, bone of our bone, and flesh of our flesh, and we are jealous that any one should be as much delighted or as thoroughly acquainted with their beauties as ourselves. For which of his poetical heroines would the reader break a lance so soon as for Jeanie Deans? What *Lady of the Lake* can compare with the beautiful Rebecca? We believe the late Mr John Scott went to his death-bed (though a painful and premature one) with some degree of satisfaction, inasmuch as he had penned the most elaborate panegyric on the *Scotch*

---

* No! For we met with a young lady who kept a circulating library and a milliner's shop, in a watering-place in the country, who, when we inquired for the *Scotch Novels*, spoke indifferently about them, said they were 'so dry she could hardly get through them,' and recommended us to read *Agnes*. We never thought of it before; but we would venture to lay a wager that there are many other young ladies in the same situation, and who think 'Old Mortality' 'dry.'

– *Sir Walter Scott* –

Novels that had as yet appeared!—The *Epics* are not poems, so much as metrical romances. There is a glittering veil of verse thrown over the features of nature and of old romance. The deep incisions into character are 'skinned and filmed over'—the details are lost or shaped into flimsy and insipid decorum; and the truth of feeling and of circumstance is translated into a tinkling sound, a tinsel *commonplace*. It must be owned, there is a power in true poetry that lifts the mind from the ground of reality to a higher sphere, that penetrates the inert, scattered, incoherent materials presented to it, and by a force and inspiration of its own, melts and moulds them into sublimity and beauty. But Sir Walter (we contend, under correction) has not this creative impulse, this plastic power, this capacity of reacting on his first impressions. He is a learned, a literal, a *matter-of-fact* expounder of truth or fable:* he does not soar above and look down upon his subject, imparting his own lofty views and feelings to his descriptions of nature—he relies upon it, is raised by it, is one with it, or he is nothing. A poet is essentially a *maker*; that is, he must atone for what he loses in individuality and local resemblance by the energies and resources of his own mind. The writer of whom we speak is deficient in these last. He has either not the faculty or not the will to impregnate his subject by an effort of pure invention. The execution also is much upon a par with the more

* Just as Cobbett is a matter-of-fact reasoner.

ephemeral effusions of the press. It is light, agreeable, effeminate, diffuse. Sir Walter's Muse is a *Modern Antique.* The smooth, glossy texture of his verse contrasts happily with the quaint, uncouth, rugged materials of which it is composed; and takes away any appearance of heaviness or harshness from the body of local traditions and obsolete costume. We see grim knights and iron armour; but then they are woven in silk with a careless, delicate hand, and have the softness of flowers. The poet's figures might be compared to old tapestries copied on the finest velvet:—they are not like Raphael's *Cartoons,* but they are very like Mr Westall's drawings, which accompany, and are intended to illustrate them. This facility and grace of execution is the more remarkable, as a story goes that not long before the appearance of the *Lay of the Last Minstrel* Sir Walter (then Mr) Scott, having, in the company of a friend, to cross the Firth of Forth in a ferry-boat, they proposed to beguile the time by writing a number of verses on a given subject, and that at the end of an hour's hard study, they found they had produced only six lines between them. 'It is plain,' said the unconscious author to his fellow-labourer, 'that you and I need never think of getting our living by writing poetry!' In a year or so after this, he set to work, and poured out quarto upon quarto, as if they had been drops of water. As to the rest, and compared with true and great poets, our Scottish Minstrel is but 'a metre ballad-monger.' We would rather have written one song of Burns, or a sin-

— *Sir Walter Scott* —

gle passage in Lord Byron's *Heaven and Earth*, or one of Wordsworth's 'fancies and good-nights,' than all his epics. What is he to Spenser, over whose immortal, ever-amiable verse beauty hovers and trembles, and who has shed the purple light of Fancy, from his ambrosial wings, over all nature? What is there of the might of Milton, whose head is canopied in the blue serene, and who takes us to sit with him there? What is there (in his ambling rhymes) of the deep pathos of Chaucer? Or of the o'er-informing power of Shakespear, whose eye, watching alike the minutest traces of characters and the strongest movements of passion, 'glances from heaven to earth, from earth to heaven,' and with the lambent flame of genius playing round each object, lights up the universe in a robe of its own radiance? Sir Walter has no voluntary power of combination: all his associations (as we said before) are those of habit or of tradition. He is a mere narrative and descriptive poet, garrulous of the old time. The definition of his poetry is a pleasing superficiality.

Not so of his NOVELS AND ROMANCES. There we turn over a new leaf—another and the same—the same in matter, but in form, in power how different! The Author of Waverley has got rid of the tagging of rhymes, the eking out of syllables, the supplying of epithets, the colours of style, the grouping of his characters, and the regular march of events, and comes to the point at once, and strikes at the heart of his subject, without dismay and without disguise. His poetry was a lady's waiting-maid, dressed out in cast-off finery: his prose is a beautiful, rustic nymph that, like Dorothea in *Don Quixote*, when she is surprised with dishevelled tresses bathing her naked feet in the brook, looks round her, abashed at the admiration her charms have excited! The grand secret of the author's success in these latter productions is that he has completely got rid of the trammels of authorship; and torn off at one rent (as Lord Peter got rid of so many yards of lace in the *Tale of a Tub*) all the ornaments of fine writing and worn-out sentimentality. All is fresh, as from the hand of nature: by going a century or two back and laying the scene in a remote and uncultivated district, all becomes new and startling in the present advanced period.—Highland manners, characters, scenery, superstitions, Northern dialect and costume, the wars, the religion, and politics of the sixteenth and seventeenth centuries, give a charming and wholesome relief to the fastidious refinement and 'over-laboured lassitude' of modern readers, like the effect of plunging a nervous valetudinarian into a cold bath. The *Scotch Novels*, for this reason, are not so much admired in Scotland as in England. The contrast, the transition is less striking. From the top of the Calton Hill, the inhabitants of 'Auld Reekie' can descry, or fancy they descry, the peaks of Ben Lomond and the waving outline of Rob Roy's country: we who live at the southern extremity of the island can only catch a glimpse of the billowy scene in the descriptions of the Author of Waverley. The mountain air is

— *Sir Walter Scott* —

most bracing to our languid nerves, and it is brought us in ship-loads from the neighbourhood of Abbotsford. There is another circumstance to be taken into the account. In Edinburgh there is a little opposition and something of the spirit of cabal between the partisans of works proceeding from Mr Constable's and Mr Blackwood's shops. Mr Constable gives the highest prices; but being the Whig bookseller, it is grudged that he should do so. An attempt is therefore made to transfer a certain share of popularity to the second-rate Scotch novels, 'the embryo fry, the little airy of *ricketty* children,' issuing through Mr Blackwood's shop-door. This operates a diversion, which does not affect us here. The Author of Waverley wears the palm of legendary lore alone. Sir Walter may, indeed, surfeit us: his imitators make us sick! It may be asked, it has been asked, 'Have we no materials for romance in England? Must we look to Scotland for a supply of whatever is original and striking in this kind?' And we answer—'Yes!' Every foot of soil is with us worked up: nearly every movement of the social machine is calculable. We have no room left for violent catastrophes; for grotesque quaintnesses; for wizard spells. The last skirts of ignorance and barbarism are seen hovering (in Sir Walter's pages) over the Border. We have, it is true, gipsies in this country as well as at the cairn of Derncleugh: but they live under clipped hedges, and repose in camp-beds, and do not perch on crags, like eagles, or take shelter, like sea-mews, in basaltic subterranean

— ALL THAT IS WORTH REMEMBERING —

caverns. We have heaths with rude heaps of stones upon them: but no existing superstition converts them into the Geese of Micklestane Moor, or sees a Black Dwarf groping among them. We have sects in religion: but the only thing sublime or ridiculous in that way is Mr Irving, the Caledonian preacher, who 'comes like a satyr staring from the woods, and yet speaks like an orator!' We had a Parson Adams not quite a hundred years ago—a Sir Roger de Coverley rather more than a hundred! Even Sir Walter is ordinarily obliged to pitch his angle (strong as the hook is) a hundred miles to the North of the 'Modern Athens' or a century back. His last work,* indeed, is mystical, is romantic in nothing but the title-page. Instead of 'a holy-water sprinkle dipped in dew,' he has given us a fashionable watering-place—and we see what he has made of it. He must not come down from his fastnesses in traditional barbarism and native rusticity: the level, the littleness, the frippery of modern civilization will undo him as it has undone us!

Sir Walter has found out (oh, rare discovery) that facts are better than fiction; that there is no romance like the romance of real life; and that if we can but arrive at what men feel, do, and say in striking and singular situations, the result will be 'more lively, audible, and full of vent,' than the fine-spun cobwebs of the brain. With reverence be it spoken, he is like the man

---

* *St Ronan's Well.*

— *Sir Walter Scott* —

who having to imitate the squeaking of a pig upon the stage, brought the animal under his coat with him. Our author has conjured up the actual people he has to deal with, or as much as he could get of them, in 'their habits as they lived.' He has ransacked old chronicles, and poured the contents upon his page; he has squeezed out musty records; he has consulted wayfaring pilgrims, bed-rid sibyls; he has invoked the spirits of the air; he has conversed with the living and the dead, and let them tell their story their own way; and by borrowing of others, has enriched his own genius with everlasting variety, truth, and freedom. He has taken his materials from the original, authentic sources, in large concrete masses, and not tampered with or too much frittered them away. He is only the amanuensis of truth and history. It is impossible to say how fine his writings in consequence are, unless we could describe how fine nature is. All that portion of the history of his country that he has touched upon (wide as the scope is) the manners, the personages, the events, the scenery, lives over again in his volumes. Nothing is wanting— the illusion is complete. There is a hurtling in the air, a trampling of feet upon the ground, as these perfect representations of human character or fanciful belief come thronging back upon our imaginations. We will merely recall a few of the subjects of his pencil to the reader's recollection; for nothing we could add, by way of note or commendation, could make the impression more vivid.

— ALL THAT IS WORTH REMEMBERING —

There is (first and foremost, because the earliest of our acquaintance) the Baron of Bradwardine, stately, kind-hearted, whimsical, pedantic; and Flora Mac-Ivor (whom even *we* forgive for her Jacobitism), the fierce Vich Ian Vohr, and Evan Dhu, constant in death, and Davie Gellatly roasting his eggs or turning his rhymes with restless volubility, and the two stag-hounds that met Waverley, as fine as ever Titian painted, or Paul Veronese:—then there is old Balfour of Burley, brandishing his sword and his Bible with fire-eyed fury, trying a fall with the insolent, gigantic Bothwell at the 'Change-house, and vanquishing him at the noble battle of Loudon-hill; there is Bothwell himself, drawn to the life, proud, cruel, selfish, profligate, but with the love-letters of the gentle Alice (written thirty years before), and his verses to her memory, found in his pocket after his death: in the same volume of *Old Mortality* is that lone figure, like a figure in Scripture, of the woman sitting on the stone at the turning to the mountain, to warn Burley that there is a lion in his path; and the fawning Claverhouse, beautiful as a panther, smooth-looking, blood-spotted; and the fanatics, Macbriar and Mucklewrath, crazed with zeal and sufferings; and the inflexible Morton, and the faithful Edith, who refused to 'give her hand to another while her heart was with her lover in the deep and dead sea.' And in *The Heart of Mid Lothian* we have Effie Deans (that sweet, faded flower) and Jeanie, her more than sister, and old David Deans, the patriarch of St Leonard's Crags, and Butler,

— *Sir Walter Scott* —

and Dumbiedikes, eloquent in his silence, and Mr Bartoline Saddletree and his prudent helpmate, and Porteous swinging in the wind, and Madge Wildfire, full of finery and madness, and her ghastly mother.—Again, there is Meg Merrilies, standing on her rock, stretched on her bier with 'her head to the east,' and Dirk Hatterick (equal to Shakespear's Master Barnardine), and Glossin, the soul of an attorney, and Dandy Dinmont, with his terrier-pack and his pony Dumple, and the fiery Colonel Mannering, and the modish old counsellor Pleydell, and Dominie Sampson,* and Rob Roy (like the eagle in his eyry), and Baillie Nicol Jarvie, and the inimitable Major Galbraith, and Rashleigh Osbaldistone, and Die Vernon, the best of secret-keepers; and in the *Antiquary*, the ingenious and abstruse Mr Jonathan Oldbuck, and the old beadsman Edie Ochiltree, and that preternatural figure of old Edith Elspeith, a living shadow, in whom the lamp of life had been long extinguished, had it not been fed by remorse and 'thick-coming' recollections; and that striking picture of the effects of feudal tyranny and fiendish pride, the unhappy Earl of Glenallan; and the Black Dwarf, and his friend Habbie of the Heughfoot (the cheerful hunter), and his cousin Grace Armstrong, fresh and laughing like the morning; and the *Children of the Mist*, and the baying of the bloodhound that tracks their steps at a distance (the hollow echoes are in our ears now), and

* Perhaps the finest scene in all these novels, is that where the Dominie meets his pupil, Miss Lucy, the morning after her brother's arrival.

Amy and her hapless love, and the villain Varney, and the deep voice of George of Douglas—and the immoveable Balafre, and Master Oliver the Barber in *Quentin Durward*—and the quaint humour of *The Fortunes of Nigel*, and the comic spirit of *Peveril of the Peak*—and the fine old English romance of *Ivanhoe*. What a list of names! What a host of associations! What a thing is human life! What a power is that of genius! What a world of thought and feeling is thus rescued from oblivion! How many hours of heartfelt satisfaction has our author given to the gay and thoughtless! How many sad hearts has he soothed in pain and solitude! It is no wonder that the public repay with lengthened applause and gratitude the pleasure they receive. He writes as fast as they can read, and he does not write himself down. He is always in the public eye, and we do not tire of him. His worst is better than any other person's best. His *backgrounds* (and his later works are little else but backgrounds capitally made out) are more attractive than the principal figures and most complicated actions of other writers. His works (taken together) are almost like a new edition of human nature. This is indeed to be an author!

The political bearing of the *Scotch Novels* has been a considerable recommendation to them. They are a relief to the mind, rarefied as it has been with modern philosophy, and heated with ultra-radicalism. At a time also, when we bid fair to revive the principles of the Stuarts, it is interesting to bring us acquainted with their persons and misfortunes. The candour of Sir Walter's historic pen levels our bristling prejudices on this score, and sees fair play between Roundheads and Cavaliers, between Protestant and Papist. He is a writer reconciling all the diversities of human nature to the reader. He does not enter into the distinctions of hostile sects or parties, but treats of the strength or the infirmity of the human mind, of the virtues or vices of the human breast, as they are to be found blended in the whole race of mankind. Nothing can show more handsomely or be more gallantly executed. There was a talk at one time that our author was about to take Guy Faux for the subject of one of his novels, in order to put a more liberal and humane construction on the Gunpowder Plot than our 'No Popery' prejudices have hitherto permitted. Sir Walter is a professed *clarifier* of the age from the vulgar and still lurking old-English antipathy to Popery and Slavery. Through some odd process of *servile* logic, it should seem, that in restoring the claims of the Stuarts by the courtesy of romance, the House of Brunswick are more firmly seated in point of fact, and the Bourbons, by collateral reasoning, become legitimate! In any other point of view, we cannot possibly conceive how Sir Walter imagines 'he has done something to revive the declining spirit of loyalty' by these novels. His loyalty is founded on *would-be* treason: he props the actual throne by the shadow of rebellion. Does he really think of making us enamoured of the 'good old times' by the faithful and harrowing portraits he has drawn of them? Would he carry us back to the early stages of barbarism, of clanship, of the feudal system as 'a consummation devoutly to be wished?' Is he infatuated enough, or does he so dote and drivel over his own slothful and self-willed prejudices, as to believe that he will make a single convert to the beauty of Legitimacy, that is, of lawless power and savage bigotry, when he himself is obliged to apologise for the horrors he describes, and even render his descriptions credible to the modern reader by referring to the authentic history of these delectable times?* He is indeed so besotted as to the moral of his own story, that he has even the blindness to go out of his way to have a fling

---

* 'And here we cannot but think it necessary to offer some better proof than the incidents of an idle tale, to vindicate the melancholy representation of manners which has been just laid before the reader. It is grievous to think that those valiant Barons, to whose stand against the crown the liberties of England were indebted for their existence, should themselves have been such dreadful oppressors, and capable of excesses, contrary not only to the laws of England, but to those of nature and humanity. But alas! we have only to extract from the industrious Henry one of those numerous passages which he has collected from contemporary historians, to prove that fiction itself can hardly reach the dark reality of the horrors of the period.

'The description given by the author of the Saxon Chronicle of the cruelties exercised in the reign of King Stephen by the great barons and lords of castles, who were all Normans, affords a strong proof of the excesses of which they were capable when their passions were inflamed. "They grievously oppressed the poor people by building castles; and when they were built, they filled them with wicked men or rather devils, who seized both men and women who they imagined had any money, threw them into prison, and put them to more cruel tortures than the martyrs ever endured. They suffocated some in mud,

— *Sir Walter Scott* —

at *flints* and *dungs* (the contemptible ingredients, as he would have us believe, of a modern rabble) at the very time when he is describing a mob of the twelfth century—a mob (one should think) after the writer's own heart, without one particle of modern philosophy or revolutionary politics in their composition, who were to a man, to a hair, just what priests, and kings, and nobles *let* them be, and who were collected to witness (a spectacle proper to the times) the burning of the lovely Rebecca at a stake for a sorceress, because she was a Jewess, beautiful and innocent, and the consequent victim of insane bigotry and unbridled profligacy. And it is at this moment (when the heart is kindled and bursting with indignation at the revolting abuses of self-constituted power) that Sir Walter *stops the press* to have a sneer at the people, and to put a spoke (as he thinks) in the wheel of upstart innovation! This is what he 'calls backing his friends'—it is thus he administers charms and philtres to our love of Legitimacy, makes us conceive a horror of all reform, civil, political, or religious, and would fain put down the *Spirit of the Age*. The Author of Waverley might just as well get up and make a speech at a dinner at Edinburgh, abusing Mr McAdam for his improvements in

---

and suspended others by the feet, or the head, or the thumbs, kindling fires below them. They squeezed the heads of some with knotted cords till they pierced their brains, while they threw others into dungeons swarming with serpents, snakes, and toads." But it would be cruel to put the reader to the pain of perusing the remainder of the description.'—*Henry's Hist.* edit. 1805, vol. vii. p.346.

— ALL THAT IS WORTH REMEMBERING —

the roads, on the ground that they were nearly *impassable* in many places 'sixty years since;' or object to Mr Peel's Police-Bill, by insisting that Hounslow Heath was formerly a scene of greater interest and terror to highwaymen and travellers, and cut a greater figure in the *Newgate Calendar* than it does at present.—Oh! Wycliffe, Luther, Hampden, Sidney, Somers, mistaken Whigs, and thoughtless Reformers in religion and politics, and all ye, whether poets or philosophers, heroes or sages, inventors of arts or sciences, patriots, benefactors of the human race, enlighteners and civilisers of the world, who have (so far) reduced opinion to reason, and power to law, who are the cause that we no longer burn witches and heretics at slow fires, that the thumbscrews are no longer applied by ghastly, smiling judges, to extort confession of imputed crimes from sufferers for conscience sake; that men are no longer strung up like acorns on trees without judge or jury, or hunted like wild beasts through thickets and glens, who have abated the cruelty of priests, the pride of nobles, the divinity of kings in former times; to whom we owe it, that we no longer wear round our necks the collar of Gurth the swineherd, and of Wamba the jester; that the castles of great lords are no longer the dens of banditti, from whence they issue with fire and sword to lay waste the land; that we no longer expire in loathsome dungeons without knowing the cause, or have our right hands struck off for raising them in self-defence against wanton insult; that we can sleep with-

— *Sir Walter Scott* —

out fear of being burnt in our beds, or travel without making our wills; that no Amy Robsarts are thrown down trap-doors by Richard Varneys with impunity; that no Red Reiver of Westburn-Flat sets fire to peaceful cottages; that no Claverhouse signs cold-blooded death-warrants in sport; that we have no Tristan the Hermit, or Petit-André, crawling near us, like spiders, and making our flesh creep, and our hearts sicken within us at every moment of our lives—ye who have produced this change in the face of nature and society, return to earth once more, and beg pardon of Sir Walter and his patrons, who sigh at not being able to undo all that you have done! Leaving this question, there are two other remarks which we wished to make on the Novels. The one was, to express our admiration of the good-nature of the mottos, in which the author has taken occasion to remember and quote almost every living author (whether illustrious or obscure) but himself—an indirect argument in favour of the general opinion as to the source from which they spring—and the other was, to hint our astonishment at the innumerable and incessant instances of bad and slovenly English in them, more, we believe, than in any other works now printed. We should think the writer could not possibly read the manuscript after he has once written it, or overlook the press.

If there were a writer, who 'born for the universe'—

— ALL THAT IS WORTH REMEMBERING —

'—Narrow'd his mind,
And to party gave up what was meant for mankind—'

who, from the height of his genius looking abroad into nature, and scanning the recesses of the human heart, 'winked and shut his apprehension up' to every thought or purpose that tended to the future good of mankind—who, raised by affluence, the reward of successful industry, and by the voice of fame above the want of any but the most honourable patronage, stooped to the unworthy arts of adulation, and abetted the views of the great with the pettifogging feelings of the meanest dependant on office—who, having secured the admiration of the public (with the probable reversion of immortality), showed no respect for himself, for that genius that had raised him to distinction, for that nature which he trampled under foot—who, amiable, frank, friendly, manly in private life, was seized with the dotage of age and the fury of a woman, the instant politics were concerned—who reserved all his candour and comprehensiveness of view for history, and vented his littleness, pique, resentment, bigotry, and intolerance on his contemporaries—who took the wrong side, and defended it by unfair means—who, the moment his own interest or the prejudices of others interfered, seemed to forget all that was due to the pride of intellect, to the sense of manhood—who, praised, admired by men of all parties alike, repaid the public liberality by striking a secret and envenomed blow at

— *Sir Walter Scott* —

the reputation of every one who was not the ready tool of power—who strewed the slime of rankling malice and mercenary scorn over the bud and promise of genius, because it was not fostered in the hot-bed of corruption, or warped by the trammels of servility—who supported the worst abuses of authority in the worst spirit—who joined a gang of desperadoes to spread calumny, contempt, infamy, wherever they were merited by honesty or talent on a different side—who officiously undertook to decide public questions by private insinuations, to prop the throne by nicknames, and the altar by lies—who being (by common consent), the finest, the most humane and accomplished writer of his age, associated himself with and encouraged the lowest panders of a venal press; deluging, nauseating the public mind with the offal and garbage of Billingsgate abuse and vulgar *slang*; showing no remorse, no relenting or compassion towards the victims of this nefarious and organized system of party-proscription, carried on under the mask of literary criticism and fair discussion, insulting the misfortunes of some, and trampling on the early grave of others—

> 'Who would not grieve if such a man there be?
> Who would not weep if Atticus were he?'

But we believe there is no other age or country of the world (but ours), in which such genius could have been so degraded!

– The New School of Reform –

A dialogue between a rationalist and a sentimentalist

> Composed by 11 February 1826; first published in *The Plain Speaker* (1826), from which the text here is reproduced. This is a defence of Hazlitt's philosophy against the hard-headed rationalism of the Utilitarians. Hazlitt was not only Bentham's tenant, but his next-door neighbour, and must have seen Bentham on numerous occasions from his house; however, the two men never met. Instead Hazlitt attacked Bentham's ally and business partner, Robert Owen; opposed Bentham's plans to build a school in the back garden; and attacked Bentham's acolyte, Francis Place, the radical tailor of Charing Cross, for having prevented Hobhouse from winning the Westminster election of 1819. This essay imagines the criticisms made of Hazlitt by the Utilitarians and responds in typically uncompromising terms.

R. What is it you so particularly object to this school? Is there any thing so very obnoxious in the doctrine of Utility, which they profess? Or in the design to bring about the greatest possible good by the most efficacious and disinterested means?

S. Disinterested enough, indeed: since their plan seems to be to sacrifice every individual comfort for

— *The New School of Reform* —

the good of the whole. Can they find out no better way of making human life run smooth and pleasant, than by drying up the brain and curdling the blood? I do not want society to resemble a *Living Skeleton,* whatever these 'Job's Comforters' may do. They are like the fox in the fable—they have no feeling themselves, and would persuade others to do without it. Take away the *dulce* of the poet, and I do not see what is to become of the *utile.* It is the common error of the human mind, of forgetting the end in the means.

R. I see you are at your *Sentimentalities* again. Pray, tell me, is it not their having applied this epithet to some of your favourite speculations, that has excited this sudden burst of spleen against them?

S. At least I cannot retort this phrase on those printed *circulars* which they throw down areas and fasten under knockers. But pass on for that. Answer me then, what is there agreeable or ornamental in human life that they do not explode with fanatic rage? What is there sordid and cynical that they do not eagerly catch at? What is there that delights others that does not disgust them? What that disgusts others with which they are not delighted? I cannot think that this is owing to philosophy, but to a sinister bias of mind; inasmuch as a marked deficiency of temper is a more obvious way of accounting for certain things than an entire superiority of understanding. The Ascetics of old thought they were doing God good service by tormenting themselves and denying others the most innocent amusements. Who doubts now that in this (armed as they were with texts and authorities and awful denunciations) they were really actuated by a morose and envious disposition, that had no capacity for enjoyment itself or felt a malicious repugnance to the idea of it in any one else? What in them took the garb of religion, with us puts on the semblance of philosophy; and instead of dooming the heedless and refractory to hell-fire or the terrors of purgatory, our modern polemics set their disciples in the stocks of Utility, or throw all the elegant arts and amiable impulses of humanity into the Limbo of Political Economy.

R. I cannot conceive what possible connection there can be between the weak and mischievous enthusiasts you speak of, and the most enlightened reasoners of the nineteenth century. They would laugh at such a comparison.

S. Self-knowledge is the last thing which I should lay to the charge of *soi-disant* philosophers; but a man may be a bigot without a particle of religion, a monk or an Inquisitor in a plain coat and professing the most liberal opinions.

R. You still deal, as usual, in idle sarcasms and flimsy generalities. Will you descend to particulars, and state facts before you draw inferences from them?

S. In the first place then, they are mostly Scotchmen—lineal descendants of the Covenanters and Cameronians, and inspired with the true John Knox zeal

— *The New School of Reform* —

for mutilating and defacing the carved work of the sanctuary—

R. Hold, hold—this is vulgar prejudice and personality—

S. But it's the fact, and I thought you called for facts. Do you imagine if I hear a fellow in Scotland abusing the Author of Waverley, who has five hundred hearts beating in his bosom, because there is no religion in his works, and a fellow in Westminster doing the same thing because there is no Political Economy in them, that any thing will prevent me from supposing that this is virtually the same Scotch pedlar with his pack of Utility at his back, whether he deals in tape and stays or in drawling compilations of history and reviews?

R. I did not know you had such an affection for Sir Walter——

S. I said the *Author of Waverley.* Not to like him would be not to love myself or human nature, of which he has given so many interesting specimens: though for the sake of that same human nature, I have no liking to Sir Walter. Those 'few and recent writers,' on the contrary, who by their own account 'have discovered the true principles of the greatest happiness to the greatest numbers,' are easily reconciled to the Tory and the bigot, because they here feel a certain superiority over him; but they cannot forgive the great historian of life and manners, because he has enlarged our sympathy with human happiness beyond their pragmatical limits.

They are not even 'good haters:' for they hate not what degrades and afflicts, but what consoles and elevates the mind. Their plan is to *block out* human happiness wherever they see a practicable opening to it.

R. But perhaps their notions of happiness differ from yours. They think it should be regulated by the doctrine of Utility. Whatever is incompatible with this, they regard as spurious and false, and scorn all base compromises and temporary palliatives.

S. Yes; just as the religious fanatic thinks there is no salvation out of the pale of his own communion, and damns without scruple every appearance of virtue and piety beyond it. Poor David Deans! how would he have been surprised to see all his follies—his 'right-hand defections and his left-hand compliances,' and his contempt for human learning, blossom again in a knot of sophists and professed *illuminés!* Such persons are not to be treated as philosophers and metaphysicians, but as conceited sectaries and ignorant mechanics. In neither case is the intolerant and proscribing spirit a deduction of pure reason, indifferent to consequences, but the dictate of presumption, prejudice, and spiritual pride, or a strong desire in the ELECT to narrow the privilege of salvation to as small a circle as possible, and in 'a few and recent writers' to have the whole field of happiness and argument to themselves. The enthusiasts of old did all they could to strike the present existence from under our feet to give us another—to annihilate our natural affections and worldly

— *The New School of Reform* —

vanities, so as to conform us to the likeness of God: the modern sciolists offer us Utopia in lieu of our actual enjoyments; for warm flesh and blood would give us a head of clay and a heart of steel, and conform us to their own likeness—'a consummation not very devoutly to be wished!' Where is the use of getting rid of the trammels of superstition and slavery, if we are immediately to be handed over to these new ferrets and inspectors of a *Police-Philosophy*; who pay domiciliary visits to the human mind, catechise an expression, impale a sentiment, put every enjoyment to the rack, leave you not a moment's ease or respite, and imprison all the faculties in a round of cant-phrases—the Shibboleth of a party? They are far from indulging or even tolerating the strain of exulting enthusiasm expressed by Spenser:—

> 'What more felicity can fall to creature
> Than to enjoy delight with liberty,
> And to be lord of all the works of nature?
> To reign in the air from earth to highest sky,
> To feed on flowers and weeds of glorious feature,
> To taste whatever thing doth please the eye?
> Who rests not pleased with such happiness,
> Well worthy he to taste of wretchedness!'

Without air or light, they grope their way underground, till they are made 'fierce with dark keeping:'*

---

*Lord Bacon, in speaking of the Schoolmen.

their attention, confined to the same dry, hard, mechanical subjects, which they have not the power nor the will to exchange for others, frets and corrodes; and soured and disappointed, they wreak their spite and mortification on all around them.

R. I cannot but think your imagination runs away with your candour. Surely the writers you are so ready to inveigh against labour hard to correct errors and reform grievances.

S. Yes; because the one affords exercise for their vanity, and the other for their spleen. They are attracted by the odour of abuses, and regale on fancied imperfections. But do you suppose they like any thing else better than they do the Government? Are they on any better terms with their own families or friends? Do they not make the lives of every one they come near a torment to them, with their pedantic notions and captious egotism? Do they not quarrel with their neighbours, placard their opponents, supplant those on their own side of the question? Are they not equally at war with the rich and the poor? And having failed (for the present) in their project of *cashiering kings*, do they not give scope to their troublesome, overbearing humour, by taking upon them to *snub* and lecture the poor *gratis*? Do they not wish to extend 'the greatest happiness to the greatest numbers,' by putting a stop to population—to relieve distress by withholding charity, to remedy disease by shutting up hospitals? Is it not a part of their favourite scheme, their nostrum, their panacea, to prevent the

— *The New School of Reform* —

miseries and casualties of human life by extinguishing it in the birth? Do they not exult in the thought (and revile others who do not agree to it) of plucking the crutch from the cripple, and tearing off the bandages from the agonized limb? Is it thus they would gain converts, or make an effectual stand against acknowledged abuses, by holding up a picture of the opposite side, the most sordid, squalid, harsh, and repulsive, that narrow reasoning, a want of imagination, and a profusion of bile can make it? There is not enough of evil already in the world, but we must harden our feelings against the miseries that daily, hourly, present themselves to our notice, and set our faces against every thing that promises to afford any one the least gratification or pleasure. This is their *idea of a perfect commonwealth*: where each member performs his part in the machine, taking care of himself, and no more concerned about his neighbours, than the iron and wood-work, the pegs and nails in a spinning-jenny. Good screw! good wedge! good tenpenny nail! Are they really in earnest, or are they bribed, partly by their interests, partly by the unfortunate bias of their minds, to play the game into the adversary's hands? It looks like it; and the Government give them 'good *oeillades*'—Mr Blackwood pats them on the back—Mr Canning grants an interview and plays the amiable—Mr Hobhouse keeps the peace. One of them has a place at the India-House: but then nothing is said against the India-House, though the poor and pious Old Lady sweats and almost swoons at

— ALL THAT IS WORTH REMEMBERING —

the conversations which her walls are doomed to hear, but of which she is ashamed to complain. One triumph of the *School* is to throw Old Ladies into hysterics!* The obvious (I should still hope not the intentional) effect of the Westminster tactics is to put every volunteer on the same side *hors de combat,* who is not a zealot of the strictest sect of those they call Political Economists; to come behind you with dastard, cold-blooded malice, and trip up the heels of those stragglers whom their friends and patrons in the *Quarterly* have left still standing; to strip the cause of Reform (out of seeming affection to it) of every thing like a *misalliance* with elegance, taste, decency, common sense, or polite literature, (as their fellow labourers in the same vineyard had previously endeavoured to do out of acknowledged hatred)—to disgust the friends of humanity, to cheer its enemies; and for the sake of indulging their unbridled dogmatism, envy and uncharitableness, to leave nothing intermediate between the Ultra-Toryism of the courtly scribes and their own Ultra-Radicalism—between the extremes of practical wrong and impracticable right. Their, *our* antagonists will be very well satisfied with this division of the spoil:—give them the earth, and any

* This is not confined to the Westminster. A certain *Talking Potato*, (who is now one of the props of Church and State,) when he first came to this country, used to frighten some respectable old gentlewomen, who invited him to supper, by asking for a slice of the 'leg of the Saviour,' meaning a leg of Lamb; or a bit of 'the Holy Ghost pie,' meaning a pigeon-pie on the table. Ill-nature and impertinence are the same in all schools.

— *The New School of Reform* —

one who chooses may take possession of the moon for them!

R. You allude to their attacks on the *Edinburgh Review*?

S. And to their articles on Scott's Novels, on Hospitals, on National Distress, on Moore's *Life of Sheridan*, and on every subject of taste, feeling, or common humanity. Sheridan, in particular, is termed 'an unsuccessful adventurer.' How gently this Jacobin jargon will fall on ears polite! This is what they call attacking principles and sparing persons: they spare the persons indeed of men in power (who have places to give away), and attack the characters of the dead or the unsuccessful with impunity! Sheridan's brilliant talents, his genius, his wit, his political firmness (which all but they admire) draw forth no passing tribute of admiration; his errors, his misfortunes, and his death (which all but they deplore) claim no pity. This indeed would be to understand the doctrine of Utility to very little purpose, if it did not at the first touch weed from the breast every amiable weakness and imperfect virtue which had—never taken root there. But they make up for their utter want of sympathy with the excellences or failings of others by a proportionable self-sufficiency. Sheridan, Fox, and Burke were mere tyros and schoolboys in politics compared to them, who are the 'mighty land-marks of these latter times'—ignorant of those principles of 'the greatest happiness to the greatest numbers,' which *a few and recent writers* have promulgated. It is one way of raising a pure and lofty enthusiasm, as to the capacities of the human mind, to scorn all that has gone before us. Rather say, this dwelling with over-acted disgust on common frailties, and turning away with impatience from the brightest points of character, is 'a discipline of humanity,' which should be confined as much as possible to the Westminster School. Believe me, their theories and their mode of enforcing them stand in the way of reform: their philosophy is as little addressed to the head as to the heart—it is fit neither for man nor beast. It is not founded on any sympathy with the secret yearnings or higher tendencies of man's nature, but on a rankling antipathy to whatever is already best. Its object is to offend—its glory to find out and wound the tenderest part. What is not malice, is cowardice, and not candour. They attack the weak and spare the strong, to indulge their officiousness and add to their self-importance. Nothing is said in the *Westminster Review* of the treatment of Mr Buckingham by the East India Company: it might lessen the writer's *sphere of utility*, as Mr Hall goes from Leicester to Bristol *to save more souls*! They do not grapple with the rich to wrest his superfluities from him (in this they might be foiled) but trample on the poor (a safe and pick-thank office) and wrench his pittance from him with their logical instruments and lying arguments. Let their system succeed, as they pretend it would, and diffuse comfort and happiness around; and they would immediately turn against it

— *The New School of Reform* —

as effeminate, insipid, and sickly; for their tastes and understandings are too strongly braced to endure any but the most unpalatable truths and the bitterest ingredients. Their benefits are extracted by the Caesarean operation. Their happiness, in short, is that—which will never be; just as their receipt for a popular article in a newspaper or review, is one that will never be read. *Their* articles are never read, and if they are not popular, no others ought to be so. The more any flimsy stuff is read and admired, and the more service it does to the sale of a journal, so much the more does it debauch the public taste, and render it averse to their dry and solid lucubrations. This is why they complain of the patronage of my *Sentimentalities* as one of the sins of the *Edinburgh Review*; and why they themselves are determined to drench the town with the most unsavoury truths, without one drop of honey to sweeten the gall. Had they felt the least regard to the ultimate success of their principles—of 'the greatest happiness to the greatest numbers,' though giving pain might be one paramount and primary motive, they would have combined this object with something like the comfort and accommodation of their unenlightened readers.

R. I see no ground for this philippic, except in your own imagination.

S. Tell me, do they not abuse poetry, painting, music? Is it, think you, for the pain or the pleasure these things give? Or because they are without eyes, ears, imaginations? Is that an excellence in them, or the fault of these arts? Why do they treat Shakespear so cavalierly? Is there any one they would set up against him—any Sir Richard Blackmore they patronise; or do they prefer Racine, as Adam Smith did before them? Or what are we to understand?

R. I can answer for it, they do not wish to pull down Shakespear in order to set up Racine on the ruins of his reputation. They think little indeed of Racine.

S. Or of Moliere either, I suppose?

R. Not much.

S. And yet these two contributed something to 'the greatest happiness of the greatest numbers;' that is, to the amusement and delight of a whole nation for the last century and a half. But that goes for nothing in the system of Utility, which is satisfied with nothing short of the good of the whole. Such benefactors of the species as Shakespear, Racine, and Moliere, who sympathised with human character and feeling in their finest and liveliest moods, can expect little favour from 'those few and recent writers,' who scorn the Muse, and whose philosophy is a dull antithesis to human nature. Unhappy they who lived before their time! Oh! age of Louis XIV and of Charles II, ignorant of the *Je ne sais quoi* and of the *savoir vivre*! Oh! Paris built (till now) of mud! Athens, Rome, Susa, Babylon, Palmyra—barbarous structures of a barbarous period—hide your diminished heads! Ye fens and dykes of Holland, ye mines of Mexico, what are ye worth! Oh! bridges raised, palaces adorned, cities built, fields cultivated

— *The New School of Reform* —

without skill or science, how came ye to exist till now! Oh! pictures, statues, temples, altars, hearths, the poet's verse, and solemn-breathing airs, are ye not an insult on the great principles of 'a few and recent writers?' How came ye to exist without their leave? Oh! Arkwright, unacquainted with spinning-jennies! Oh, Sir Robert Peel, unversed in calico-printing! Oh! generation of upstarts, what good could have happened before your time? What ill can happen after it?

R. But at least you must allow the importance of first principles?

S. Much as I respect a dealer in marine stores, in old rags and iron: both the goods and the principles are generally stolen. I see advertised in the papers—'Elements of Political Economy, by James Mill,' and 'Principles of Political Economy, by John Macculloch.' Will you tell me in this case, whose are the First Principles? which is the true Simon Pure?

> 'Strange! that such difference there should be
> 'Twixt *Tweedle-dum* and *Tweedle-dee!*'

R. You know we make it a rule to discountenance every attempt at wit, as much as the world in general abhors a punster.

S. By your using the phrase, 'attempts at wit,' it would seem that you admit there is a true and a false wit; then why do you confound the distinction? Is this logical, or even politic?

— ALL THAT IS WORTH REMEMBERING —

R. The difference is not worth attending to.

S. Still, I suppose, you have a great deal of this quality, if you chose to exert it?

R. I fancy not much.

S. And yet you take upon you to despise it! I have sometimes thought that the great professors of the modern philosophy were hardly sincere in the contempt they express for poetry, painting, music, and the Fine Arts in general—that they were private *amateurs* and prodigious proficients *under the rose*, and, like other lovers, hid their passion as a weakness—that Mr Mill turned a barrel-organ—that Mr Peacock warbled delightfully—that Mr Place had a manuscript tragedy by him, called 'The Last Man,' which he withheld from the public, not to compromise the dignity of philosophy by affording any one the smallest actual satisfaction during the term of his natural life.

R. Oh, no! you are quite mistaken in this supposition, if you are at all serious in it. So far from being proficients, or having wasted their time in these trifling pursuits, I believe not one of the persons you have named has the least taste or capacity for them, or any idea corresponding to them, except Mr Bentham, who is fond of music, and says, with his usual *bonhommie* (which seems to increase with his age) that he does not see why others should not find an agreeable recreation in poetry and painting.*

---

* One of them has printed a poem entitled 'Rhodope;' which, however, does not show the least taste or capacity for poetry, or any idea

— *The New School of Reform* —

S. You are sure this cynical humour of theirs is not affectation, at least?

R. I am quite sure of it.

S. Then I am sure it is intolerable presumption in them to think their want of taste and knowledge qualifies them to judge (*ex cathedrâ*) of these Arts; or is a standard by which to measure the degree of interest which others do or ought to take in them. It is the height of impertinence, mixed up with a worse principle. As to the excesses or caprices of posthumous fame, like other commodities, it soon finds its level in the market. *Detur optimo* is a tolerably general rule. It is not of forced or factitious growth. People would not trouble their heads about Shakespear, if he had given them no pleasure, or cry him up to the skies, if he had not first raised them there. The world are not grateful *for nothing.* Shakespear, it is true, had the misfortune to be born before our time, and is not one of 'those few and recent writers,' who monopolize all true greatness and wisdom (though not the reputation of it) to themselves. He need not, however, be treated with contumely on this account: the instance might be passed over as a solitary one. We shall have a thousand Political Economists, before we have another Shakespear.

---

corresponding to it. *Bad poetry* serves to prove the existence of *good.* If all poetry were like *Rhodope,* the philosophic author might fulminate his anathemas against it (floods of ghastly, livid ire) as long as he pleased: but if this were poetry, there would be no occasion for so much anger: no one would read it or think any thing of it!

R. Your mode of arriving at conclusions is very different, I confess, from the one to which I have been accustomed, and is too wild and desultory for me to follow it. Allow me to ask in my turn, Do you not admit Utility to be the test of morals, as Reason is the test of Utility?

S. Pray, what definition have you (in the School) of Reason and of Utility?

R. Nay, they require no definition; the meaning of both is obvious.

S. Indeed, it is easy to dogmatize without definitions, and to repeat broad assertions without understanding them. Nothing is so convenient as to begin with gravely assuming our own infallibility, and we can then utter nothing but oracles, of course.

R. What is it *you* understand by Reason?

S. It is your business to answer the question; but still, if you choose, I will take the *onus* upon myself, and interpret for you.

R. I have no objection, if you do it fairly.

S. You shall yourself be judge. Reason, with most people, means their own opinion; and I do not find your friends a particular exception to the rule. Their dogmatical tone, their arrogance, their supercilious treatment of the pretensions of others, their vulgar conceit and satisfaction in their own peculiar tenets, so far from convincing me that they are right, convince me that they must be wrong (except by accident, or by mechanically parrotting others); for no one ever

— *The New School of Reform* —

thought for himself, or looked attentively at truth and nature, that did not feel his own insufficiency and the difficulty and delicacy of his task. Self-knowledge is the first step to wisdom. The *Rational Dissenters* (who took this title as a characteristic distinction, and who professed an entire superiority over prejudice and superstition of all sorts,) were as little disposed to have their opinions called in question as any people I ever knew. One of their preachers thanked God publicly for having given them a *liberal religion.* So your School thank God in their hearts for having given them a *liberal philosophy*: though what with them passes for liberal is considered by the rest of the world as very much akin to illiberality.

R. May I beseech you to come to the point at once?

S. We shall be there soon enough, without hurrying. Reason, I conceive, in the sense that you would appeal to it, may signify any one of three things, all of them insufficient as tests and standards of moral sentiment, or (if that word displeases) of moral conduct:—1. Abstract truth, as distinct from local impressions or individual partialities; 2. Calm, inflexible self-will, as distinct from passion; 3. Dry matter of fact or reality, as distinct from sentimentality or poetry.

R. Let me hear your objections; but do for once adhere to the track you have chalked out.

S. 'Thereafter as it happens.' You may drag your grating go-cart of crude assumptions and heavy paralogisms along your narrow iron railway, if you please:

but let me diverge down 'primrose paths,' or break my neck over precipices, as I think proper.

R. Take your own course. *A wilful man must have his way.* You demur, if I apprehend you right, to founding moral rectitude on the mere dictates of the Understanding. This I grant to be the grand *arcanum* of the doctrine of Utility. I desire to know what other foundation for morals you will find so solid?

S. I know of none so flimsy. What! would you suspend all the natural and private affections on the mere logical deductions of the Understanding, and exenterate the former of all the force, tenderness, and constancy they derive from habit, local nearness or immediate sympathy, because the last are contrary to the speculative reason of the thing? I am afraid such a speculative morality will end in speculation, or in something worse. Am I to feel no more for a friend or a relative (say) than for an inhabitant of China or of the Moon, because, as a matter of argument, or setting aside their connection with me, and considered absolutely in themselves, the objects are, perhaps, of equal value? Or am I to screw myself up to feel as much for the Antipodes (or God knows who) as for my next-door neighbours, by such a forced intellectual scale? The last is impossible; and the result of the attempt will be to make the balance even by a diminution of our natural sensibility, instead of an universal and unlimited enlargement of our philosophic benevolence. The feelings cannot be made to keep pace with our bare knowledge of existence or

— *The New School of Reform* —

of truth; nor can the affections be disjoined from the impressions of time, place, and circumstance, without destroying their vital principle. Yet, without the sense of pleasure and pain, I do not see what becomes of the theory of Utility, which first reduces every thing to pleasure and pain, and then tramples upon and crushes these by its own sovereign will. The effect of this system is, like the touch of the torpedo, to chill and paralyse. We, notwithstanding, find persons acting upon it with exemplary coolness and self-complacency. One of these 'subtilised savages' informs another who drops into his shop that news is come of the death of his eldest daughter, adding, as matter of boast—'I am the only person in the house who will eat any dinner today: *they do not understand the doctrine of Utility!*' I perceive this illustration is not quite to your taste.

R. Is it any thing more than the old doctrine of the Stoics?

S. I thought the system had been wholly new—the notable project of a 'few and recent writers.' I could furnish you with another parallel passage in the HYPOCRITE.*

---

* '*Old Lady Lambert.* Come, come: I wish you would follow Dr Cantwell's precepts, whose practice is conformable to what he teaches. Virtuous man!—above all sensual regards, he considers the world merely as a collection of dirt and pebblestones. How has he weaned me from temporal connexions! My heart is now set upon nothing sublunary; and, I thank Heaven, I am so insensible to every thing in this vile world, that I could see you, my son, my daughters, my brothers, my grandchildren, all expire before me, and mind it no more than the going out of so many snuffs of a candle.

R. Is it not as well, on any system, to suppress the indulgence of inordinate grief and violent passion, that is as useless to the dead as it is hurtful to the living?

S. If we could indulge our affections while they run on smoothly, and discard them from our breasts the instant they fail of their objects, it might be well. But the feelings, the habitual and rooted sentiments of the soul, are not the creatures of choice or of a fanciful theory. To take the utmost possible interest in an object, and be utterly and instantaneously indifferent to the loss of it, is not exactly in the order of human nature. We may blunt or extirpate our feelings altogether with proper study and pains, by ill-humour, conceit, and affectation, but not make them the playthings of a verbal paradox. I fancy if Mr —— had lost a hundred pounds by a bad debt, or if a lump of soot had fallen into his broth, it would have spoiled his dinner. The doctrine of Utility would not have come to his aid here. It is reserved for great and trying occasions; or serves as an excuse for not affecting grief which its professors do not feel. So much for reason against passion.

R. But if they do not possess all the softness and endearing charities of private life, they have the firmness and unflinching hardihood of patriotism and devotion to the public cause.

'*Charlotte.* Upon my word, madam, it is a very humane disposition you have been able to arrive at, and your family is much obliged to the Doctor for his instructions.'— Act II, Scene I.

— *The New School of Reform* —

S. That is what I have yet to learn. They are a kind of Ishmaelites, whose hand is *against* others—what or who they are for (except themselves) I do not know. They do not willingly come forward into the front nor even show themselves in the rear of the battle, but are very ready to denounce and disable those who are indiscreet enough to do so. They are not for precipitating a crisis, but for laying down certain general principles, which will do posterity a world of good and themselves no harm. They are a sort of *occult* reformers, and patriots *incognito.* They get snug places under Government, and mar popular Elections—but it is to advance the good of the cause. Their theories are as whole and as sleek as their skins, but that there is a certain jejuneness and poverty in both which prevents their ever putting on a wholesome or comfortable appearance.

R. But at least you will not pretend to deny the distinction (you just now hinted at) between things of real Utility and merely fanciful interest?

S. No, I admit that distinction to the full. I only wish you and others not to mistake it.

R. I have not the slightest guess at what you mean.

S. Is there any possible view of the subject that has not been canvassed over and over again in the *School*? Or do you pass over all possible objections as the dreams of idle enthusiasts? Let me ask, have you not a current dislike to any thing in the shape of sentiment or *sentimentality*? for with you they are the same. Yet a thing and the *cant* about it are not the same. The cant about Utility does not destroy its essence. What do you mean by *sentimentality*?

R. I do not know.

S. Well: you complain, however, that things of the greatest use in reality are not always of the greatest importance in an imaginary and romantic point of view?

R. Certainly; this is the very pivot of all our well-grounded censure and dissatisfaction with poetry, novel-writing, and other things of that flimsy, unmeaning stamp.

S. It appears, then, that there are two standards of value and modes of appreciation in human life, the one practical, the other ideal,—that that which is of the greatest moment to the Understanding is often of little or none at all to the Fancy, and *vice versa.* Why then force these two standards into one? Or make the Understanding judge of what belongs to the Fancy, any more than the Fancy judge of what belongs to the Understanding? Poetry would make bad mathematics, mathematics bad poetry: why jumble them together? Leave things, that are so, separate. *Cuique tribuito suum.*

R. I do not yet comprehend your precise drift.

S. Nay, then, you will not. It is granted that a certain thing, in itself highly useful, does not afford as much pleasure to the imagination, or excite as much interest as it ought to do, or as some other thing which is of less real and practical value. But why *ought* it to

— *The New School of Reform* —

excite this degree of interest, if it is not its nature to do so? Why not set it down to its proper account of Utility in any philosophical estimate—let it go for what it is worth there, *valeat quantum valet*—and let the other less worthy and (if you will) more meretricious object be left free to produce all the sentiment and emotion it is capable of, and which the former is inadequate to, and its value be estimated accordingly!

R. Will you favour me with an illustration—with any thing like common sense?

S. A table, a chair, a fire-shovel, a Dutch-stove are useful things, but they do not excite much sentiment—they are not confessedly the poetry of human life.

R. No.

S. Why then endeavour to make them so; or in other words, to make them more than they are or can become? A lute, a sonnet, a picture, the sound of distant bells can and do excite an emotion, do appeal to the fancy and the heart (excuse this antiquated phraseology!)—why then grudge them the pleasure they give to the human mind, and which it seems, on the very face of the argument, your objects of mere downright Utility (which are not also objects of Imagination) cannot? Why must I come to your shop, though you expressly tell me you have not the article I want? Or why swear, with Lord Peter in the *Tale of a Tub*, that your loaf of brown bread answers all the purposes of mutton? Why deprive life of what cheers and adorns, more than of what supports it? A chair is good to sit in (as a matter of fact), a table to write on, a fire to warm one's self by—No one disputes it; but at the same time I want something else to amuse and occupy my mind, something that stirs the breath of fancy, something that but to think of is to feel an interest in. Besides my automatic existence, I have another, a sentimental one, which must be nourished and supplied with proper food. This end the mere circumstance of practical or real Utility does not answer, and therefore is so far good for nothing.

R. But is it not to be feared that this preference should be carried to excess, and that the essential should be neglected for the frivolous?

S. I see no disposition in mankind to neglect the essential. Necessity has no choice. They pursue the mechanical mechanically, as *puss* places herself by the fireside, and snuffs up the warmth:—they dream over the romantic; and when their dreams are golden ones, it is pity to disturb them. There is as little danger as possible of excess here; for the interest in things merely *ideal* can be only in proportion to the pleasure, that is, the real benefit which attends them. A calculation of consequences may deceive, the impulses of passion may hurry us away: sentiment alone is infallible, since it centres and reposes on itself. Like mercy, 'its quality is not strained: it droppeth as the gentle dew from heaven upon the place beneath!'—

R. You have asked me what Reason is: may I ask you what it is that constitutes Sentiment?

— *The New School of Reform* —

S. I have told you what Reason is: you should tell me what Sentiment is. Or I will give your learned professors and profound Encyclopedists, who lay down laws for the human mind without knowing any of the springs by which it acts, five years to make even a tolerable guess at what it is in objects that produces the fine flower of Sentiment, and what it is that leaves only the husk and stalk of Utility behind it.

R. They are much obliged to you, but I fancy their time is better employed.

S. What! in ringing the changes on the same cant-phrases, one after the other, in newspapers, reviews, lectures, octavo volumes, examinations, and pamphlets, and seeing no more of the matter all the while than a blind horse in a mill?

R. I have already protested against this personality. But surely you would not put fiction on a par with reality?

S. My good friend, let me give you an instance of my way of thinking on this point. I met Dignum (the singer) in the street the other day: he was humming a tune; and his eye, though quenched, was smiling. I could scarcely forbear going up to speak to him. Why so? I had seen him in the year 1792 (the first time I ever was at a play), with Suett and Miss Romanzini and some others, in No Song No Supper; and ever since, that bright vision of my childhood has played round my fancy with unabated, vivid delight. Yet the whole was fictitious, your cynic philosophers will say. I wish there were but a few realities that lasted so long, and were followed with so little disappointment. The *imaginary* is what we conceive to be: it is reality that tantalizes us and turns out a fiction—that is the false Florimel!

R. But the Political Economists, in directing the attention to 'the greatest happiness of the greatest numbers,' wish to provide for the solid comforts and amelioration of human life.

S. Yes, in a very notable way, after their fashion. I should not expect from men who are jealous of the mention of any thing like enjoyment, any great anxiety about its solid comforts. Theirs is a very comfortable theory indeed! They would starve the poor outright, reduce their wages to what is barely necessary to keep them alive, and if they cannot work, refuse them a morsel for charity. If you hint at any other remedy but 'the grinding law of necessity' suspended *in terrorem* over the poor, they are in agonies and think their victims are escaping them: if you talk of the pressure of Debt and Taxes, they regard you as a very commonplace person indeed, and say they can show you cases in the reign of Edward III where, without any reference to Debt or Taxes, the price of labour was tripled—after a plague! So full is their imagination of this desolating doctrine, that sees no hope of good but in cutting off the species, that they fly to a pestilence as a resource against all our difficulties—if we had but a pestilence, it would demonstrate all their theories!

— *The New School of Reform* —

R. Leave Political Economy to those who profess it, and come back to your mystical metaphysics. Do you not place actual sensations before sentimental refinements, and think the former the first things to be attended to in a sound moral system?

S. I place the heart in the centre of my moral system, and the senses and the understanding are its two extremities. You leave nothing but gross, material objects as the ends of pursuit, and the dry, formal calculations of the understanding as the means of ensuring them. Is this enough? Is man a mere animal, or a mere machine for philosophical experiments? All that is intermediate between these two is sentiment: I do not wonder you sometimes feel a *vacuum,* which you endeavour to fill up with spleen and misanthropy. Can you divest the mind of habit, memory, imagination, foresight, will? Can you make it go on physical sensations, or on abstract reason alone? Not without making it over again. As it is constituted, reflection recalls what sense has once embodied; imagination weaves a thousand associations round it, time endears, regret, hope, fear, innumerable shapes of uncertain good still hover near it. I hear the sound of village bells—it 'opens all the cells where memory slept'—I see a well-known prospect, my eyes are dim with manifold recollections. What say you? Am I only as a rational being to hear the sound, to see the object with my bodily sense? Is all the rest to be dissolved as an empty delusion, by the potent spell of unsparing philosophy? Or rather, have not a thousand

— ALL THAT IS WORTH REMEMBERING —

real feelings and incidents hung upon these impressions, of which such dim traces and doubtful suggestions are all that is left? And is it not better that truth and nature should speak this imperfect but heartfelt language, than be entirely dumb? And should we not preserve and cherish this precious link that connects together the finer essence of our past and future being by some expressive symbol, rather than suffer all that cheers and sustains life to fall into the dregs of material sensations and blindfold ignorance? There, now, is half a definition of Sentiment: for the other half we must wait till we see the article in the Scotch Encyclopedia on the subject. To deprive man of sentiment, is to deprive him of all that is interesting to himself or others, except the present object and a routine of cant-phrases, and to turn him into a savage, an automaton, or a Political Economist. Nay more, if we are to feel or do nothing for which we cannot assign a precise reason, why we cannot so much as walk, speak, hear, or see, without the same unconscious, implicit faith—not a word, not a sentence but hangs together by a number of imperceptible links, and is a bundle of prejudices and abstractions.

R. I can make nothing of you or your arguments.

S. All I would say is, that you cannot take the measure of human nature with a pair of compasses or a slip of parchment: nor do I think it an auspicious opening to the new *Political Millennium* to begin with setting our faces against all that has hitherto kindled the

— *The New School of Reform* —

enthusiasm, or shutting the door against all that may in future give pleasure to the world. Your Elysium resembles Dante's *Inferno*—'Who enters there must leave all hope behind!'

R. The poets have spoiled you for all rational and sober views of men and society.

S. I had rather be wrong with them, than right with some other persons that I could mention. I do not think you have shewn much tact or consecutiveness of reasoning in your defence of the system: but you have only to transcribe the trite arguments on the subject, set your own and a bookseller's name to them, and pass off for the head of a school and one of the great lights of the age!

– London Solitude –

> First published *The Atlas*, 28 March 1830, the version reproduced here. Hazlitt did not grow up in London, but it was his adopted home and he celebrated it many times in print before writing this farewell. Although Hazlitt did feel alone in his poverty and sickness, he was a sociable man frequently in company even during his last months. He died surrounded by a small but loyal group of friends.

In London anything may be had for money; and one thing may be had there in perfection without it. That one thing is solitude. Take up your abode in the deepest glen, or on the wildest heath, in the remotest province of the kingdom, where the din of commerce is not heard, and where the wheels of pleasure make no trace, even there humanity will find you, and sympathy, under some of its varied aspects, will creep beneath the humble roof. Travellers' curiosity will be excited to gaze upon the recluse, or the village pastor will come to offer his religious consolations to the heart-chilled solitary, or some kind spinster who is good to the poor, will proffer her kindly aid in medicine for sickness, or in some shape of relief for poverty. But in the mighty metropolis, where myriads of human hearts are

— *London Solitude* —

throbbing—where all that is busy in commerce, all that is elegant in manners, all that is mighty in power, all that is dazzling in splendour, all that is brilliant in genius, all that is benevolent in feeling, is congregated together—there the pennyless solitary may feel the depth of his solitude. From morn to night he may pensively pace the streets, envying every equipage that sweeps by him in its pride, and coveting the crusts of the unwashed artificer. And there shall pass him in his walks poets that musically sing of human feeling, priests that preach the religion of mercy, the wealthy who pity the sorrows of the poor, the sentimental whose hearts are touched by the tale of woe—and none of these shall heed him; and he may retire at night to his bedless garret, and sit cold and hungry by his empty grate; the world may be busy and cheerful and noisy around him, but no sympathy shall reach him; his heart shall be dry as GIDEON'S fleece while the softening dews of humanity are falling around him.

– Party Spirit –

First published *The Atlas*, 25 April 1830, the version given here. Hazlitt's fascination with political and religious difference was a life-long preoccupation; in this essay he traces factionalism to the incorrigible love of tribal affiliation he had often noted among the English (in 'Character of John Bull', for instance).

April 25, 1830

Party spirit is one of the *profoundnesses of Satan,* or in more modern language, one of the dexterous *equivoques* and contrivances of our self-love, to prove that we, and those who agree with us, combine all that is excellent and praiseworthy in our own persons (as in a ring-fence) and that all the vices and deformity of human nature take refuge with those who differ from us. It is extending and fortifying the principle of the *amour-propre*, by calling to its aid the *esprit de corps* and screening and surrounding our favourite propensities and obstinate caprices in the hollow squares or dense phalanxes of sects and parties. This is a happy mode of pampering our self-complacency, and persuading ourselves that we and those that side with us, are 'the salt of the earth'; of giving vent to the morbid

— *Party Spirit* —

humours of our pride, envy, and all uncharitableness, those natural secretions of the human heart, under the pretext of self-defence, the public safety, or a voice from Heaven, as it may happen; and of heaping every excellence into one scale, and throwing all the obloquy and contempt into the other, in virtue of a nick-name, a watch-word of party, a badge, the colour of a ribbon, the cut of a dress. We thus desolate the globe, or tear a country in pieces, to show that we are the only people fit to live in it; and fancy ourselves angels, while we are playing the devil. In this manner, the Huron devours the Iroquois, because he is an Iroquois, and the Iroquois the Huron for a similar reason; neither suspects that he does it, because he himself is a savage and no better than a wild beast; and is convinced in his own breast that the difference of name and tribe makes a total difference in the case. The Papist persecutes the Protestant, the Protestant persecutes the Papist in his turn; and each fancies that he has a plenary right to do so, while he keeps in view only the offensive epithet which 'cuts the common link of brotherhood between them.' The church of England ill-treated the Dissenters, and the Dissenters, when they had the opportunity, did not spare the church of England. The Whig calls the Tory a knave, the Tory compliments the Whig with the same title, and each thinks the abuse sticks to the party-name, and has nothing to do with himself or the generic name of *man*. On the contrary, it cuts both ways; but while the Whig says 'The Tory is a knave, because he is a Tory,' this is as much as to say, 'I cannot be a knave, because I am a Whig'; and by exaggerating the profligacy of his opponent, he imagines he is laying the sure foundation, and raising the lofty superstructure of his own praises. But if he says, which is the truth, 'The Tory is not a rascal because he is a Tory, but because human nature in power, and with the temptation, is a rascal,' then this would imply that the seeds of depravity are sown in his own bosom, and might shoot out into full growth and luxuriance if he got into place, which he does not wish to appear *till he does get into place.*

We may be intolerant even in advocating the cause of Toleration, and so bent on making proselytes to free-thinking as to allow no one to think freely but ourselves. The most boundless liberality in appearance may amount in reality to the most monstrous ostracism of opinion—not in condemning this or that tenet, or standing up for this or that sect or party, but in assuming a supercilious superiority to all sects and parties alike, and proscribing in the lump and in one sweeping clause all arts, sciences, opinions, and pursuits but our own. Till the time of Locke and Toland a general toleration was never dreamt of: it was thought right on all hands to punish and discountenance heretics and schismatics, but each party alternately claimed to be true Christians and orthodox believers. Daniel Defoe, who spent his whole life, and wasted his strength in asserting the right of the Dissenters to a toleration

— *Party Spirit* —

(and got no thanks for it but the pillory), was scandalized at the proposal of the general principle, and was equally strenuous in excluding Quakers, Anabaptists, Socinians, Sceptics, and all who did not agree in the *essentials* of Christianity, that is, who did not agree with him, from the benefit of such an indulgence to tender consciences. We wonder at the cruelties formerly practised upon the Jews: is there anything wonderful in it? They were at the time the only people to make a butt and a bugbear of, to set up as a mark of indignity and as a foil to our self-love, for the *feræ naturæ* principle that is within us and always craving its prey to hunt down, to worry and make sport of at discretion, and without mercy—the unvarying uniformity and implicit faith of the Catholic church had imposed silence, and put a curb on our jarring dissensions, heart-burnings, and ill-blood, so that we had no pretence for quarrelling among ourselves for the glory of God or the salvation of men:—a Jordanus Bruno, an atheist or sorcerer, once in a way, would hardly suffice to stay the stomach of our theological rancour, we therefore fell with might and main upon the Jews as a *forlorn hope* in this dearth of objects of spite or zeal; or, as the whole of Europe was reconciled in the bosom of holy mother church, went to the holy land in search of a difference of opinion and a ground of mortal offence; but no sooner was there a division of the Christian world than Papist fell upon Protestant, Protestants upon schismatics, and schismatics upon one another, with the same loving fury as they had before fallen upon Turks and Jews. The disposition is always there, like a muzzled mastiff—the pretext only is wanting; and this is furnished by a name, which, as soon as it is affixed to different sects or parties, gives us a license, we think, to let loose upon them all our malevolence, domineering humour, love of power and wanton mischief, as if they were of different species. The sentiment of the pious English bishop was good, who, on seeing a criminal led to execution, exclaimed, 'There goes my wicked self!'

If we look at common patriotism, it will furnish an illustration of party-spirit. One would think by an Englishman's hatred of the French, and his readiness to die fighting with and for his countrymen, that all the nation were united as one man in heart and hand—and so they are in wartime—and as an exercise of their loyalty and courage; but let the crisis be over, and they cool wonderfully, begin to feel the distinctions of English, Irish, and Scotch, fall out among themselves upon some minor distinction; the same hand that was eager to shed the blood of a Frenchman will not give a crust of bread or a cup of cold water to a fellow-countryman in distress; and the heroes who defended the wooden walls of Old England are left to expose their wounds and crippled limbs to gain a pittance from the passenger, or to perish of hunger, cold, and neglect in our highways. Such is the effect of our boasted nationality: it is active, fierce in doing mischief; dormant, lukewarm in doing good. We may also see why the greatest stress is laid on trifles in religion, and why the most violent animosities arise out of the smallest differences in politics and religion. In the first place, it would never do to establish our superiority over others by the acquisition of greater virtues, or by discarding our vices; but it is charming to do this by merely repeating a different *formula* of prayer, or turning to the east instead of the west. He should fight boldly for such a distinction, who is persuaded it will furnish him with a passport to the other world, and entitle him to look down on the rest of his fellows as *given over to perdition.* Secondly, we often hate those most with whom we have only a slight shade of difference, whether in politics or religion; because as the whole is a contest for precedence and infallibility, we find it more difficult to draw the line of distinction where so many points are conceded, and are staggered in our conviction by the arguments of those whom we cannot despise as totally and incorrigibly in the wrong. The high-church party in Queen Anne's time were disposed to sacrifice the low church and Dissenters to the Papists, because they were more galled by their arguments and disconcerted with their pretensions. In private life, the reverse of the foregoing reasoning holds good; that is, trades and professions present a direct contrast to sects and parties. A conformity in sentiment strengthens our party and opinion; but those who have a similarity of pursuit are rivals in interest; and hence the old maxim, that *two of a trade cannot agree.*

Notting Hill Editions

Notting Hill Editions is devoted to the best in essay writing. Our authors, living and dead, cover a broad range of non-fiction, but all display the virtues of brevity, soul and wit.

Our commitment to reinvigorating the essay as a literary form extends to our website, where we host the wonderful Essay Library, a home for the world's most important and enjoyable essays, including the facility to search, save your favourites and add your comments and suggestions.

To discover more, please visit
www.nottinghilleditions.com